The Art of Picasso

Sue Matynia

First published in Australia in September 2023
by Sue Matynia 2023
Sue Matynia has asserted her right under the Copyright,
Deigns and Patents Act, 1988, to be identified as Author of
this work.
https://socialobservingbysue.com.au

This work is copyright. Apart from any use as permitted under
the Copyright Act 1968, no part may be reproduced, copied,
scanned, stored in a retrieval system, recorded, or transmitted,
in any form or any means, without the prior written
permission of the publisher or author. A catalogue record for
this book is available from the National Library of Australia

ISBN 978-0-6459024-0-2 (paperback)
ISBN 978-0-6459024-1-9 (ebook)

Cover design by Sue Matynia and Chrissy McYoung
Author Photograph by Leisha Cox
https://leighsacoxphtographer.com.au

Typesetting by Rack and Rune Publishing
https://rackandrune.com

*For Big Bro, who guided me to look at life in different perspectives,
and to the young people who said, 'I just want someone to listen.'*

'You never really know someone until you step in their shoes and walk around.'
Atticus Finch 'To Kill a Mockingbird'
(Harper Lee)

Forepaw:

Stop doing things on the tap tap machine. It's time to go. The little black dog was impatient and used her two front paws to shove Sara's calves.

'What is it? What do you want?' Sara exhaled.

I know what you're doing, and it's not work. You're playing that game thing again, aren't you? The little black dog angrily stared at Sara.

'I am working, see? Typing,' Sara explained.

I can tell when it is normal typing and play typing. If you want to play, we need to go outside and play or go for a walk. The little black dog scolded and made another forceful shove on Sara's calves.

'Okay, so I was playing solitaire for a bit, but I am working now. See all the words on the page? I'm making good progress.' Sara knew that she has been caught out.

I don't believe you. I want you to write about me, the black dog dictated.

'This is Big Bro's story; you're still living and cannot be written about yet' Sara complained.

No, write about me. Now, we either go for a walk and then come back and work, or we go straight to work. And no playing games on the tap tap machine. The little black dog was direct with her instruction.

'Okay, we'll start again, although I really do object to your manner, and your forceful shoves on my legs.' Sara had lost this point.

It's my story and what I say goes. Start typing what I say. I will let you add things when I see fit. Okay, start, now. The little black dog gave one more shove to Sara's calves.

The little black dog stared Sara down. Chihuahuas are known for their steadfast determination. Sara sighed and returned to her laptop, patiently typing out her argumentative companion's story as instructed:

Chapter 1: Bush Beginnings

A crisp winter's morning shone on the melting frost patches that looked eerily white against the dull green tufts. A tiny ramshackle shearer's cottage sat forlornly in the middle of a paddock at Brokenrock. The cottage's wooden frame had sagged in various places, and makeshift supports helped to prop up the rickety veranda. Extra rooms of all sizes and shapes had been tacked on the back of the cottage at some stage. A crooked black chimney chugged out smoke.

The peaceful country scenery gave no hint as to the chaos taking place inside the cottage. A lone dog charged into the cottage via the lean-to and joined in the action. Bedlam had been unleashed as the two people inside began running back and forth. Three dogs, six puppies, two cats, and parrots and budgies in cages were screaming 'breakfast' in their own way. The warmth of the wood-burning fire permeated the two front rooms where most of the critters (both domesticated and wild) had congregated. Several years of 'comfort' were presented in all rooms of the cottage. Mismatched furniture seemed to satisfy all needs, piles of newspaper lay precariously stacked, and shoes, pet toys, magazines, blankets and other assortments showed age and a need for a good clean. The animals made as much racket and mess as possible as they tried to navigate through the maze of furniture, papers and other such items.

The little puppies were continually running into things, toppling over furniture and sending papers flying, all of which overwhelmed the cottage's human inhabitants.

Morning rest time came quickly to the little family of puppies snuggling up to their Jack Russell mother. The puppies all found their special spot and soon were fast asleep. The Chihuahua father looked over his brood as they slept on the old chair with the broken springs.

The only home the puppies knew would soon be shattered. Visitors regularly arrived and then left with a puppy.

Not me, I'm staying here. I'm not going to be taken away to a strange place, the littlest one promised herself and hid each time a car pulled into the yard.

'Nobody wants this one, the runt of the litter, Kay. She can't stay here any longer. I'll have to find a home for her,' Doug admitted as he scratched his stubbly chin and patted down his long sideburns. Tall and gangly, he always wore his terry cloth hat to hide his bald spot.

'Here, wrap her in this blanket and put her in the cardboard box. Don't come back tonight if she is still with you. I can't stand any more of this. I'm too tired to look after all these animals any longer.' Kay dropped her plump figure into the chair, wiping her forehead with her handkerchief. Kay was wearing a typical housewife dress with a flower-patterned apron. She placed her handkerchief back in the apron's pocket, raised her sturdily clad feet on the ottoman and closed her eyes.

Thinking cuddles and food were coming, the puppy was easy for Doug to catch. He placed her in the box on the car seat next to him and folded himself into the small, compact car. He puttered through the property gates and waited at the main road for a break in traffic before turning right towards the town. During the twenty-minute drive, he planned his attempt to give the puppy away. Kay had meant business when she said, 'Don't come back tonight if she is still with you.'

Doug arrived at his cousin's house first. The cousin greeted him with a shake of his head.

He tried to give the puppy to the veterinarian's adoption program.

He tried to give the puppy to his friends.

He wandered down the street, talking and showing all the shoppers what was in the box. But he had no luck.

He then had a spark of an idea, and drove towards the nursery on top of the hill.

Doug thought, 'Tony's always kind and has a stray cat at the back of the shop, perhaps he will take her?'

'Hey Tony, nice to see you looking good. How's business today?' Doug greeted his friend.

'Hi Doug. It's good today. Lots of people doing over their gardens, lots of mulch and gardening tools sold. I've done a quote on old George's place – he wants to redo his retaining wall, keeps things going at this time of year.' Tony was chuffed with himself as his thick black moustache twitched.

Tony was tall, not as tall as Doug, but had a big barrel chest that made him look powerful. He had thick wavy and wiry black hair with several grey hairs thrown in that stuck out in odd places. The contrast with his large white teeth and tanned skin made for an unmistakable package. His thick arms, hands and fingers looked purposely built for working on the land and landscaping. He would blend in very well in an Italian rural setting tending an olive grove.

'Happy for yah. I've got something to show you, cute as, and so robust. Be a great addition to anyone's home.' Doug chirped.

Doug went back to his car, crouched inside and brought out the cardboard box with the puppy and showed Tony. Tony's face fell, but his eyes misted over. There was a very small black dog with enormous eyes and ears, and a tan face and chest staring up at him.

'Oh no, my missus will kill me if I bring it home. She said no more – we already have enough mouths to feed. Can't take it.' Tony took a step away and shook his head, his wiry hair accentuated with the head shake.

'She's only small. She was born at the beginning of June and doesn't eat much. She will never get very big. Tell you what, you keep her for a month, see if she settles in, and if she does not, I'll take her back. Yah gotta help me. Kay will kill me if I come home with it,' Doug pleaded.

Tony agreed to take the dog on 'trial', knowing full well he would never give it back.

Chapter 2: A New Family

The puppy travelled in her cardboard box to Scotsfield - which was another small township in the country, not as isolated as Brokenrock - and a much more modern house. Tony proudly showed Sara the cardboard box with the little black puppy.

'What do you mean? You have the dog on trial? No! More! Animals! We have enough. I've already told you this. Take her back,' the words spurted like spitfire from Sara's mouth. Sara shook her head, her brown spiky hair quivering at the top, hands on her hips and feet planted apart. Sara only came up to Tony's shoulders, but had a ferocious spirit to her. Tony knew this stance too well, but kept it up.

'But honey, Kay will kill Doug if he brings her home,' whimpered Tony, his moustache forming a perfect 'o'.

'Like I'm gonna kill you? Then this is not a trial. I want nothing to do with it. YOU do all the hard yakka with the puppy. It's YOUR stuff up, YOU do the work.' Steam could be seen escaping from Sara's nostrils and ears.

If Sara's eyes had been lasers and could burn holes into people, Tony would be no more. Luckily, Tony was used to this look and turned his back.

Tony took the puppy out of the box and let her run in the lounge.

Many smells of other animals were already there, so the puppy knew she was not alone. Greeting her was a reddish-brown kelpie dog with a tan face and chest that she soon knew as 'Big Bro.'

Hi, Big Bro. It's nice to meet you. Do you have any other brothers or sisters? The puppy looked around eagerly.

Yes, they are outside at the moment. We only stay in this half of the house. The other bits are for our humans, Sara and Tony. The most important part we need to know is this area, which they name 'the kitchen.' It contains all the best things. Food comes out of here on a regular basis, so this is my favourite place, Big Bro explained. There were so many new rules to learn, but over time Big Bro would guide her through these complex routines.

We all leave our birth family for a new one. This is my third family and I think I will keep this one. It is the best so far. Big Bro beamed.

I miss my old home and family. I gotta lie down. The little puppy curled into a tight ball and was soon asleep.

I know, Little One, it takes some time to adjust. I will look over you and keep you safe from harm. The Kelpie sat next to the sleeping little dog.

Tony put the puppy's cardboard box on a towel next to the door and out of the way, especially out of Sara's way. Tony lifted the sleeping puppy and placed her in the box. The puppy did not wake. This was the puppy's new sleeping area.

'She'll cool down in a few weeks, Big Bro. Just make sure the puppy does the right thing.' Tony patted Big Bro's head.

A short time later the puppy woke, yawned, stretched and stumbled out of her box. She then squatted on the carpet, relieving herself.

No, Little One, not there. It must be done outside. If Sara and Tony see this, they will freak. We have to take our business outside. Big Bro tried to hide the wet patch as he tugged the box over it.

What? I had to go. I feel better. Play time. The puppy pranced excitedly and started to explore her new home. Nose to the floor, the puppy sniffed every inch of her new area. Each sniff uncovered many more hidden surprises and she tried to follow the pattern of who or what had made these smells. Staring up, she saw two grey striped animals slightly bigger than herself. Thinking these were some of her brothers or sisters, she bounced up to them in greeting.

Hello, hello, I've missed you, so nice to see you again, she prattled.

The two grey heads turned in the direction of the little black dog and were repulsed that this thing had found its way into the house, especially as they had just seen her messing the floor. Totally Undignified with a Capital 'U,' they decided. Out came a left hook and whack to the side of the puppy's face. Bullseye. Whack came another one, the claws only slightly retracted. The final blow from both animals scored a double whack to the head and body. The little puppy cried and retreated towards Big Bro.

Why have they done this? I was only saying hello, and they attacked me. They hurt me and kept hitting me. I want to go home to my old family. I don't like it here. I want to go. Picasso wailed and shivered.

Big Bro tried to comfort the little dog while Sara's laughter was heard from the kitchen.

'Teach the puppy right, pussy cats,' Sara snickered.

Big Bro was not impressed.

Why did you attack this poor little dog? She is missing her family and out of sorts. Do you think you could be a little kinder to her? Big Bro scolded the cats.

She's a silly dog and she messed the floor. We saw her do it. She's so 'Uncouth.' She needs to know her place in this house and who comes first. I think we have told her, Strife shot back.

Trouble and Strife, you should be more accommodating to newcomers. She has just left her birth family and is feeling lost and lonely. It is up to us to make her feel welcome and help her out. We don't want her to be upset, do we? Big Bro reasoned.

We will try, but she needs to know the rules of the house and abide by them. I cannot bear to live in a house where one member ruins everything. You keep her in check, Strife demanded of Big Bro.

Both she and her sister swaggered from the room. Sara's laughter abated. Big Bro gave Sara another angry look and returned his attention to the young puppy shaking at his paws.

It's fine now, Little One. I've told them off. They will now be kind to you. Let's hope Sara does not see your wet patch,' Big Bro soothed.

Just then, a tennis ball rolled out into the lounge from the kitchen. Big Bro pounced on the ball and squeezed it in his mouth. Another ball rolled out, this one smaller for the puppy. Before the puppy had a chance to investigate, Big Bro pounced on this one too. The little black dog cowered out of the way and watched the Kelpie's enthusiasm with balls and squeak toys. She retreated to her basket and felt safe there.

Way too scary for me. I'm safe here, in my box, it reminds me of home, I miss my family, the little black dog cowered and snuggled in her box, sucking the blanket. She continued to suck until she fell asleep, dreaming of the care and safety of her birth mother.

The puppy soon excelled at this task, sucking holes in blankets, shoes, socks and anything else lying around.

Traditional ball games and 'dog' behaviour were out for the puppy. She revelled at tearing up tissues, showing off her strength and aggression with each one. She scattered bits of tissues throughout the house. Big Bro, Trouble, Strife and Tony and Sara were puzzled, but the puppy had found her own game.

Chapter 3: Naming Day

Everybody has a name and a place in the world. Big Bro called the young puppy Little One, but she had yet to obtain a 'human' name.

Within the first few nights in her new home, the puppy extended her exploration. Ignoring Big Bro's directions, she headed for the 'banned' area of the house. She located the small shower room where both Tony and Sara were. They had newspapers on the floor, which reminded the puppy of her birth home.

'We've got to get this ceiling sanded and painted tonight. It will dry and we can do another coat before the open house on Saturday. I hope we get some good buyers out of this next lot,' Tony said from atop the ladder as splatters of peeling paint wove their way into his thick wiry hair. White dust and peeling paint rained down from the ceiling while Sara started preparing the paint.

After a light dust down, Sara handed Tony the edging brush loaded with white ceiling paint. It did not take long to cut in the job. Sara loaded the paint tray up with paint and passed the roller up to Tony while she took the brush from him. With both concentrating on the ceiling work, the new puppy wandered into the room and walked through the paint tray. Slipping and sliding on the newspapers on the floor, paint on paws splattering everywhere, the puppy tried to find a way out.

'Hey! The puppy is in here! She's got paint all over her! Grab her quick!' Tony shouted from atop the ladder. Sara grabbed the puppy around the middle just before she made it to the carpeted hallway.

'No you don't, you little rat. You're having a bath.' She held the dog at arm's length and ran towards the laundry to wash the paint from her. The puppy squirmed and kicked as hard as she could during her first bath.

I told you not to go past the hallway, Big Bro chuckled.

I will never have another bath in my life. I will run and hide, the puppy promised herself.

Sara scrubbed the paint off the puppy's feet and where it had splattered on her underside. The puppy, still kicking and fighting, was dried with a rough towel. Sara then locked both dogs in the family room and returned to the bathroom to complete the ceiling.

'Sara, look what the little dog has done, amazing pictures in a cubism or something like that genre. I know, I will call the puppy Picasso,' Tony pointed to the 'paintings' on the newspapers on the floor.

Overhearing this conversation, the puppy tried to dry her still damp fur. *What's a Picasso?*

Picasso is a famous painter in a cubism genre. I saw a program about him on ABC TV once while watching with Sara and Tony. They think we cannot see well or see colour. They think we cannot understand their world, but we do, and much better than they think we do, Big Bro hummed.

So, there is another Picasso out there? I wonder who she is and what her humans are like? Picasso continued to groom herself.

Chapter 4: Reality Bites

Big Bro shared many stories from the past as he and Picasso explored their home environment. Big Bro turned out to be more than a teacher; he was an Educator Extraordinaire. He didn't just provide yes or no answers but allowed discussion and applied deeper meanings to everyday encounters. He never preached but used his time in a mentor role to help with getting over the rough patches. Picasso followed Big Bro everywhere.

All creatures have an internal clock that tells us so many things: eating time, sleeping time, car ride time, when it's V-E-T time, or any other time of the day. For example, we can sense danger long before humans can. Humans are very slow at picking up these things, so we have to look after them. They would be lost without us, Big Bro beamed.

But if we are so good and they are so stupid, why do we keep them around? Picasso wondered.

It is essential for harmony that all things are balanced. We need differences to make all our lives wonderful. That, and our thumbs are virtually useless and cannot operate the can opener. It is also difficult to operate the fridge and freezer where all the really good food is. We could always return to our ancestral roots and be wild dogs again, but we have evolved, and are too sophisticated and domesticated for this. Therefore, we need people to gain access to our food. I think the food factories designed cans this way in order to match us up with a family.

It must be bad if dogs prefer the wild outside rather than a safe place to call home. Picasso mused.

Sometimes, it is safer for them on the streets. Believe it or not, it happens with humans as well. We never truly know all the circumstances of each other's lives. We don't know what they've been through. You never really know the full story unless you ask. Don't judge them or turn your nose up at them, treat them with respect, they probably deserve it.

Picasso was awestruck. *Wow, I guess it takes all kinds to make the world go round. What else can we help people with?*

Lots of things, Little One, lots of things.

Big Bro let his thoughts trail away as he stopped to adorn himself with plumbago flowers from the front garden, getting them entangled in the fur all over his body. Picasso was letting the thoughts of a sad home life wash over her, thankful for coming to a good home. Both dogs patrolled the rest of the garden to make sure everything was in its place. Picasso tried to dig but did not get very far in the hard clay soil base.

No, Little One, no digging allowed on the property.

Just as well, I don't want to get my feet dirty and have another bath. Hey, Big Bro. I need some help. My private bottom is very itchy. It feels like something is biting me down there. I can't make it stop. It is driving me crazy. Picasso wiped her bum on the grass.

Big Bro watched the puppy's antics of wiping and then rolling over to see if that eased the itching.

On full investigation of what you have told me, and by observing you, I suspect you might have a case of worms. This is a common ailment for us and can be easily treated. What we need to do is show Sara and Tony the problem. They will get the point if you follow what I tell you to do. Big Bro instructed Picasso on the things to do to show Tony and Sara.

Back at the house, Big Bro waited for evening television time when Sara and Tony were most relaxed in the lounge. Tony always liked looking at the home renovation shows, picking up a few trends in landscaping houses. He sat with his notepad and pen, ready to take notes.

'Old George has just had his retaining wall redone, and I noticed he had a lot of old farming implements. I convinced him to hire me to make these a feature in his backyard,' Tony eagerly stated.

'It's good that the old things are put to use in an artistic way, instead of hidden in the back of the shed,' Sara remarked as she sat with her cup of tea, ready to enjoy the program.

Big Bro patiently waited for the first commercial break to end before he gave the nod to Picasso. This should give the puppy maximum opportunity to showcase her needs. Picasso started her routine of bum-scooting across the carpeted floor, with all legs assisting in movement. A crazed look on her face completed the task as she quickly rose and tried to bite her bottom.

Tony and Sara were distracted by the puppy's antics and glanced towards the floor and the little black dog. Big Bro gave a barely audible *Harump*' and Picasso bum-scooted across the carpet again. Horrified, Sara jumped up and yelled at the dogs.

'No! No bum-scooting on the carpet. Stop this at once. I don't need to clean the carpet again before the showing. Outside with you! No.' Sara ushered both dogs outside.

They left with their heads held high.

I think they have the message. Something will happen now for your worms. Big Bro proudly huffed and chuckled as he sniffed the night air for another whiff of plumbago perfume.

I hope it comes fast, whatever it is. It's really itchy. I think I have carpet burn to add to the worms, Picasso confessed.

The next day, Tony placed some flavoured milk in a bowl for Picasso. She lapped it up so fast, licked her lips and looked around for more.

'It's chocolate flavour. This will fix you up.' Tony stood and put the medicine away.

So this is what chocolate tastes like? It is nice and I want some more. Picasso looked from her bowl to Tony and back.

Don't be greedy, just take what you need. Big Bro stopped Picasso begging for more.

Big Bro and Tony were right. The chocolate drink stopped Picasso's bum itching.

Chapter 5: Friends

Picasso made an able and willing student, absorbing most things her Big Bro told her. She also learned by watching and listening to her humans.

'Everybody must do something on a property. There is no free ride for anyone. The cows trim the grass for us, the chickens give us eggs, the cats scare the mice and rats away, and you are the supervisor, Big Bro. Make sure the eagles do not take away any of the chickens, keep this property and all inhabitants safe. But you, puppy, what good are you?' asked Sara as she continued her chores of mucking out the barn.

I am good for lots of things, but I won't tell you. You'll have to figure them out, stupid human, miffed Picasso.

Big Bro explained his job in more depth to Picasso as they slinked away from Sara, ready to do some visiting.

Most homes have an animal or three attached to the houses in this area. Next door has a horse called Jazz, there are sheep on the other side – they don't have names, and there are many dogs and cats like Ned, Bonny, Lara, Betty or D'fer in the neighbourhood.

Making friends and chatting with everyone in the neighbourhood was Big Bro's thing. Picasso took a different pathway. She dragged herself along but chose not to associate with anybody.

Hey Picasso, come and see Lara and the bunny in a hutch. Big Bro quickened his pace.

Don't want to see them. Lara doesn't talk to me and the bunny doesn't do anything. Don't know why you have to drag me around the neighbourhood, grumbled Picasso.

Oh, don't be like that. This is all about making friends and sharing things. This is what makes life a great place to be. Some don't have the luxury we do. I've suspected Lara is deaf and cannot hear like we hear. I'll show you when we visit. Watch what I do. Big Bro entered Lara's property by squeezing himself through a hole in the fence.

How did you get to learn all these things, Big Bro? Picasso easily wandered in.

It is called wisdom. Wisdom comes with age and life experience. If you go rushing into things, you will miss many things. If you carefully analyse and observe, you will see a better way. We all live in harmony with each other. We all share the same space. Therefore, we all must get along. Each of us has our own special abilities and strengths. We also have weaknesses. By using the best of what we have, we can make life better for others. None of us are perfect, but if we try to do our very best each and every day, it will make a better world and come back to us in abundance. Life is wonderful.

Like what? Tell me more.

Well, for example, when Tony and Sara get home from work, give them a few minutes to settle and change clothes before we go for a walk. They will be more accepting of doing energetic things this way. Another example could be going to a new area. Don't pee on all the grass at the beginning, save some for other places to mark to say you've been here. Another one we will test out now, with Lara. Big Bro scanned the yard for Lara.

Wow. You certainly know your stuff. How can I learn these things?

You can't learn everything out of a book or by watching TV. Sometimes life experiences mean more. Big Bro chuckled.

Chapter 6: Creative Communicating

Look! There's Lara. Watch how I move so she can see me approaching. It is best manners to announce yourself when you enter another's property. Big Bro made some slight zigzagging moves, raised his tail high and waved it like a flag, the white tip on the end of his tail very visible from a distance. Lara, a brown spotted Dalmatian cross, saw Big Bro approach and was ready to greet her friend.

Good morning Lara, it's nice to see you up and about. I hope I haven't disturbed you. This is my sister, Picasso. She's only very young and still learning. Big Bro introduced Picasso to Lara.

Lara looked from Big Bro to the little puppy. There was some connection here. Big Bro moved his mouth in speech, but the words were not understood. Lara was happy to see them nonetheless and wagged her tail. She was waiting for the next step.

See, I told you I suspect something is different about Lara. I will now test my theory out. Please stand back and take notice of what Lara does. Big Bro moved up close to Lara and rested his head against her head. Lara allowed him to do this. She trusted him and he had always been respectful to her. Big Bro filled his lungs and let out a very loud, piercing bark right beside Lara's ear. Picasso jumped.

I felt the vibrations, but I still could not hear you. I think we understand each other better now. I live in a silent world, Lara confessed.

I knew something was going on with your ears, now this confirms it. You must always use your eyes and your sense of smell to ensure you remain safe and well. I will try to teach my family how to communicate with you via body language. This might work. How does this seem to you?

If she's deaf, why are you telling her this? Picasso complained.

It's polite, that's why. Besides, she is used to talking, but not hearing, said Big Bro.

I see you trying to talk to me, but I don't understand all of the meanings. It can be frustrating not hearing. Still, it would be nice to communicate in some way. I hope you can teach me better communication. It can be a lonely world sometimes, Lara admitted.

I'm off to see the bunny before I go. I need to figure out how to train Sara and Tony and anyone else so we can talk to Lara. I think they might be trainable. Bye Lara. Come, Picasso. Big Bro wandered around the back to look at the bunny in the hutch while Picasso reluctantly followed, clearly bored with her brother's activity. She wondered what sort of plan Big Bro was devising. Sara and Tony would be in for something!

'Hi Big Bro, looking at the bunny again? Have you seen Lara?' Jenn called out from her back stairs her customary sporting clothes clung to her athletic shape.

Lara's out the front, I'll get her for you. If I can teach my people to talk to Lara, anything is possible. It's just the first step of many. Cutting his time short with the bunny, Big Bro retrieved Lara from the front and guided her to the back where Jenn was.

Here she is. Looks like it's your morning tea time, Lara. See you later. Big Bro left with Picasso.

I see what you mean by some people not understanding. Do you think you can teach ours? Picasso quizzed.

Yes, both Sara and Tony have higher intelligence for their species when it comes to communicating with animals. I think I can teach them both. Sara always picks up faster than Tony – I'll start with her.

Both dogs wandered through their neighbourhood, discussing ways to communicate with humans, and how they have managed in life without the special skills of dogs. Every blade of grass was smelt and marked as they continued the discussion of skills like, hearing, smelling and sensing.

Chapter 7: Difficulties

It's hard understanding the best way forward, the best way to live and behave. We truly never know what the other person is going through unless we step into their shoes and walk around a bit, Big Bro chatted.

What do you mean? Walk in their shoes? We don't wear shoes – we go barepaw, Picasso stated.

It's a figure of speech, just something we say to get a better understanding of the bigger picture. Big Bro felt that another long explanation was due.

How do we get a bigger picture? Picasso quizzed.

Let's go see Betty. We can try to understand more through her eyes, Big Bro decided.

Through her eyes? We can't exchange eyes. How can we do this? Picasso questioned.

This is another figure of speech, and it just means listening to others about their story, finding things out from their perspective, giving them a chance, Big Bro responded.

Sounds very confusing to me, figures of speech. Why don't we just say what we want to say? Picasso stated.

Sometimes, it is just too painful to do. Here, up here, squeeze through this gate, go slow and quiet. We don't want Betty's owners catching on, Big Bro hushed.

Why? Picasso questioned.

Shhhh, be quiet; just watch and listen, as Big Bro snuck up to the wire cage in the back yard. He scanned the yard for Betty and found her huddled near the tree. Big Bro and Picasso get as close as they could to Betty and quietly called out. It took Betty a few moments to lift her head. Betty had a very heavy chain around her neck attached to the tree. She was very dusty and deflated, her eyes glazed over, but she did recognise Big Bro at first.

Big Bro, I haven't seen you for ages, not since he moved in, as she glanced towards the house. *I can't say anything too loud – he's sleeping and I don't want to wake him up,* Betty whispered.

Hi Betty, I just wanted to say hello and introduce you to my new sister, Picasso. She has some learning to do. Big Bro introduced Picasso.

Hello Picasso. Sorry, but I can't get up, I have no energy. Betty exhaled.

Why? Picasso probed.

Everything is just too hard. For the last few months since he moved in, I have been chained in this yard. No more coming into the house or sleeping on comfy beds or blankets. I barely get enough food and my water bowl is green. He keeps telling me off for doing things, says things like 'a waste of space,' 'better off without the mutt,' even things I don't do – he blames me for everything. I knew I was a good girl, but he keeps this tirade up, so I think I am starting to believe it. I wish I were dead. This is no way to live life. I don't seem to have a life at all. Betty groaned.

Betty, you are a wonderful girl: very bright, happy and we have had lots of fun. I wish I could take you away from this miserable place. I would love you to live with us. You will be treated with the respect you deserve, Big Bro consoled.

I don't think there is any hope left for me. I think it's my time, I want to go now. Betty admitted defeat.

No, Betty, we can work on this together. You are not alone. We can get this fixed. You are a special girl with so much to give. I know it might not seem like it now, but you will have a better future, Big Bro pleaded.

Whilst Big Bro continued to talk to Betty, a large van drove into the property and parked between the house and Betty's enclosure. The van was white and had some blue on it. There were five big letters on the side, R, S, P, C, A, and some other smaller words and numbers that Big Bro could not read well enough. Two people got out, glanced at the wire cage in the back, went to the house and rapped on the door. They looked very official with their reflective shirts, big boots, a fistful of paper in their hands, leads and a long metal thing that you would find in a workshop. The man came to the door and argued with the two. Loud voices are heard. Big Bro, Picasso and Betty felt anger in the air and cowered.

Big Bro did not fully understand the conversation, but he sensed something good will happen with this visit. He heard the words 'surrender' and 'going to court,' as well as 'fines' and 'unsafe living conditions,' but still did not know their exact meaning.

The two people started heading towards Betty, holding the leads and bolt cutters, gently calling Betty's name. Betty was too scared to lift her head, thinking that she had moments left of life. The two hoomans started talking to Betty in soft and soothing voices. They seemed kind that she even attempted to stand up on her weakened legs. Her tail started a slow wiggle. A rod came out and went around Betty's neck and tightened. Betty let it happen – if this was the end, then she would be at peace. The two hoomans started moving closer to her and one undid the heavy chain around her neck with the bolt cutters. She received a few pats on the head and down her body. Some places still hurt, and she flinched.

'Hey Betty, we are going to take you away from here and give you some good food and medical care. You won't have to live here anymore – we will find a good family for you to live with. Do you want to try to walk, or should we carry you?' one of the hoomans asked.

Betty turned to Big Bro and Picasso, *Is it true? Am I going to a better place?*

Yes Betty, something good has happened and you are moving to a better place.

Please don't be sad anymore, keep looking forward to a better life. We will miss you. Big Bro urged Betty on.

Thanks Big Bro, I am hopeful for the future. I won't be sad anymore if I find a better family. I hope to have a great life. Betty slowly walked towards a better future.

Big Bro and Picasso walked back to the front of the gate and saw Betty and the two hoomans leave in the van.

Goodbye Betty, have a great life, Big Bro called out at the retreating van.

That was good luck, I think those two hoomans will bring Betty to a better place. Her circumstances were not good, Big Bro told Picasso.

It that why she was so sad and had these really bad thoughts? Picasso asked.

Perhaps. Perhaps we could have helped her more, like visiting or getting help faster. I didn't realise she was in such a bad way. This is why we have to talk to anybody and everybody. A kind word might be the only comfort someone has. You will never know unless you ask. Are you okay? Big Bro chatted on the way home.

Why didn't we know? Picasso asked

Sometimes, these things are hidden, like negativity. Negativity brings you down, puts harmful thoughts in your head. If we hear negative things all the time, we sometimes start to believe it. Don't ever believe these negative thoughts — there is always a better way. Believe in this, Big Bro advocated as they wandered home.

Chapter 8: Actions and Consequences

Hoomans are a regimented lot who focus on things called watches or clocks. These things help them get things done in the day, like getting up or eating. Have you noticed the big round thing on the kitchen wall? That's a clock. Speaking of clocks, it's time to go to my very favourite place in the house – the kitchen. It has got to be the best invention in the world. Imagine, a whole room set aside for food! Big Bro mimicked Pavlov's dog's behaviour and salivated as the aroma of home cooking wafted in the air and tempted them to the back of the house. Upon entering the kitchen, they found Sara cooking. Big Bro's whole body did his happy jig as he smelt what she was cooking.

'Oh, are you back from visiting the neighbours? Jenn phoned to say you were visiting the bunny and Lara. Did they have much to say?' Sara continued her stirring the pot on the stovetop.

Both dogs and the two cats lined up and patiently waited for any scraps. They smelt meat- mince to be exact, mince with tasty morsels put in- being cooked on the stove. There was chicken stock, and gravy, and pasta, and something else. What was it? It smelt healthy. It smelt yuck. It was green vegetables, and in fact, it was peas.

Big Bro nudged Sara and silently begged, *No peas in with the vegetables, Mum, please not. We like everything else, but not the peas. Please.*

'What is it? I'm cooking your meals, like I always do. All your favourite things are in it. Here, taste,' as Sara put a sample spoonful on a saucer for the Kelpie to inspect.

But it's got peas and other green veggies. I can smell them. Even though you've cut them up small, I can still smell and taste them. Please, not the peas, Big Bro pleaded through his licking the saucer.

'I'm putting these in to make sure you are all healthy and happy. You need a balanced diet if you are to remain well. I know you don't like peas, but I have mashed them up so you don't see the round shape. I think it's the shape you hate, but they are good for you,' Sara stated.

Big Bro retreated to the imaginary line separating the dining room from the kitchen, laid down and dropped his head on his outstretched arms. A sigh was expelled while watching the cooking process.

Why doesn't she listen to you? Why does she put all those green things in your food? Strife asked.

What, you mean, there are green things in my meals? She has been poisoning me? I'm dying. Picasso gagged and rolled on her back.

You are not dying, you silly dog. Watch the pecking order. You need to make her understand, Big Bro, Strife continued.

It doesn't matter anyway, it's still food. Trouble showed off her rotund figure.

She means well, I am sure, but I still don't like peas. Big Bro was resigned to having vegetables hidden in his food.

Where do the peas come from? Picasso asked.

All food is found in this room: this big white thing they call a fridge. The best stuff is kept in the cool part, the next best stuff is kept in the very cold part they call a freezer. This stuff needs to be heated up before eating. This is where the peas come from, Big Bro explained.

Well, if the peas come from the freeze part, why don't we destroy it? Picasso suggested.

*Little One, there are many other good things stored in there too, like meat called beef, or lamb, or chicken. We don't want to destroy that. Besides, if we destroy the *freeze section, then the cool section will not work. They belong together.* Big Bro chuckled.

'What are you lot jabbering about? Are you conspiring against me?' Sara turned and watched the interactions. Big Bro was caught with the guilty look on his face.

'I can see you were plotting something. It better not be bad,' Sara warned.

All previous discussions were now forgiven. Sara gave each animal a 'sample' taste of her homemade dog food. The cats agreed this was good, even with the peas.

I told you there are benefits of having hoomans live with us. We couldn't make something this good, could we? Big Bro licked his lips and watched over his sisters, hoping they would leave something on the saucer for him to clean up.

'See, it wasn't so bad, was it? This will make a good batch to last you several weeks.' Sara ladled the homemade dog food into smaller containers ready to freeze.

Knowing that there was no more to sample, all pets went their own separate way, ready for a nap or other activities.

So, having hoomans in our lives is good. Picasso sleepily prodded her blanket to make it fluffy enough.

Yes, Little One. Hoomans enrich our lives, and we theirs. Some can be slow, but we humour them as it makes them feel important. Their communication abilities other than speech are lacking. Therefore, we have to teach them to understand our body language. You just saw an example of it with the peas and Mum. Big Bro found his special spot on the lounge room floor and was ready for a nap. *The love and sharing we have with our hooman family make us a part of their lives,* Big Bro said.

Why did you just call Sara Mum? Picasso questioned.

This is another name we can call our loved ones. It's called an endearing name. This is when we love, care and share so much with them. It's a term of honour. There is a very special place in our hearts for our hoomans, Big Bro explained.

Huh? Picasso uttered.

I call Sara and Tony Mum and Dad as that's what they are to me. It's a term of love for them. Big Bro sighed.

Well, I can't say that yet, I had a mum and dad and they had four feet each and fur all over. When Sara and Tony grow extra feet and fur, then I might think about calling them that, Picasso stated.

Big Bro chuckled at his young apprentice's determination and forcefulness.

Is body language the same for all species? Picasso continued.

Mostly, but we each have our own special ways. For example, when we see another dog, our heads and tails are in the upright position. We are very proper in our greetings. We smell the air first to see how they are, and upon meeting we remain at the respectful distance, smelling each other's aura. Usually all is good and we can then properly greet each other, Big Bro said sleepily.

So how do you know which smells are good or bad?

Each of us smells differently and this provides so much information. If something is wrong, we will hold ourselves differently, or if we are not feeling well, we tend to sag and droop. This can be challenging if you are a Bassett Hound. Sometimes, you sense something is not right, and have to ask the tough questions to find out more. Luckily, Mum is quick to pick up on things and will be able to observe these language skills. I'll point out some of the things they are starting to pick up later tonight. Have you noticed she's starting to use her hands and arms in greeting by moving them back and forth? She tries to do a tail wag. We should try her out on Lara. Maybe she has learnt Dog Auslan.

Snickers of laughter rang out from the two dogs at the thought of Sara and Tony trying to act like dogs.

If we can educate one hooman, surely others will follow? Picasso commented.

Chapter 9: Inner Strengths

'Hey, there is a really good program on telly tonight: it's about dogs, jobs and how they pick up things around them. Might be good to have a watch, might pick up a few pointers to help with this lot.' Sara motioned to the seemingly innocent animals having a snooze.

'It always amazes me how they know things before we even think of them. I mean, if we think of giving them a treat like Smackos, they are already at the panty waiting for one. Or they always seem to know when it's time to go to the V-E-T and scarper. How do they know these things?' Tony asked.

'Well, I think it will be a good program to watch. I wonder how many secrets they don't let us in on?' Sara eyed the animals suspiciously.

More than you think, Mum, more than you think, Big Bro commented with a smirk on his face.

The family settled in for the night to watch their program on telly. Sara brought cups of tea for the two of them, while Tony worked the remote control.

I wish we could have more control of that button thing – there are so many good shows we miss during the day when they're not here, Big Bro stated.

I don't want to know, as it cuts in on my sleep time. I love my regular beauty treatment time, Trouble retorted.

It's a really hard thing to master – all those little buttons. We seem to press many of them at once, Big Bro reasoned.

I think I know how to do it. I've watched them for some time now. I've been keeping my eyes on them to know the secret and I've been practising. I'll show you when they've gone. It's really quite easy if you know how. I mean, even now they don't realise I've been watching for a long time, even though I've left them some hints. They are really slow and stupid, Strife commented.

Strife, don't say that about Mum and Dad. What if they hear you and stop your food? Big Bro told Strife off.

Don't worry, how can they know we're talking about them? And they wouldn't stop our food, Strife argued back.

Stop our food? What? NO! They wouldn't do that, would they? Trouble quivered fearfully.

No, of course not, Trouble. I'm just saying we should be kinder to those who are less intelligent or able than ourselves. It's not their fault, but assisting them to learn, such as watching this program, will hopefully educate them. We're here to help them in their life. Big Bro broke the tension.

I've grown to like the food and house here. I don't want anything to change, Picasso piped up.

The TV sprung to life and the commercial break for the station began. The station logo's set of nine balls began to tumble down and out of sight.

I love this part. I'll catch them all. Strife torpedoed towards the TV set and tried to catch the balls before they hit the floor.

Standing on her hind feet, she pawed the screen and tried to get the balls from underneath too. Chuckles of laughter were heard from Tony and Sara at the cat's antics. Even Big Bro joined in.

What's so funny? Picasso asked.

Strife always tries to catch the balls on the TV set before they fall, but they're not real. You should see when she watches a nature show with birds on it. She tries to catch them too. Big Bro chuckled.

'You should see when we watch a National Geographic show with wildlife and especially birds. Strife tries to catch them, even going behind the TV to see if they are coming out of the box,' Sara snickered.

'I was wondering why the screen is always smudged. They do make us laugh, don't they?' Tony joined in.

The program began by exploring the history of dogs, the anatomy and what makes them different from humans in the smell area. It explained that the scent glands are over four hundred times superior to humans, and how dogs can pick up a trace of scent.

Dogs with jobs can do all sorts of things, like detect missing persons in an avalanche, if a building has collapsed, or if lost in the woods, simply by their scent. Special dogs are also used for food or drug detection at security points such as airports or prisons. Dogs can also sense internal chemical imbalances in humans and can work with people with epilepsy or severe diabetes. The program also showed the relationship between the handler and the animal.

Why are they so stupid? There's more to smelling than this! And why are they only talking about dogs? Have they mentioned how impressive cats are? Strife was insulted.

Shh, Strife. I'm sure cats have the same abilities that dogs have, and a certain agility that we will never have, but we must be kind to our hoomans who are just learning about these things. We must help them on their way, Big Bro scolded.

Big Bro looked back to Sara and Tony to make sure they didn't hear this conversation. Both were absorbed on the program, although Big Bro did see Sara quickly glance his way. Perhaps she knew and understood more than she was letting on?

The program continued by highlighting the breeds best chosen for specific jobs, how they mark and follow scents, how they trace things back, and the years of training to get to that stage.

'Well, that was a good show. I certainly learned a lot from it. I wonder if we could train Big Bro to do some work?' Tony pondered.

'He's already doing enough work- keeping the cats and Picasso in line, making sure the eagles don't take our chooks away, frightening the snakes and making sure things are okay here. I'd hate him to go away for training. Besides, I think they start them young. He's too old,' Sara countered.

See, I told you they can learn if they watch the program, Big Bro proudly stated.

But they also said you were too old, Strife poked.

They know I have a busy job here to do, Big Bro puffed out his chest.

I'm young. They might send me away to training camp? Picasso offered.

Don't be silly, who would want you? What can you do? You're not a big powerful dog like a Beagle or a Labrador or an Alsatian, or a Spaniel or anything else. You're a Chihuahua crossed with something else, Strife said sarcastically.

A Jack Russell, and I'm proud of my heritage. I can do lots of things, Picasso dared Strife.

Is the program over? Snack time! Trouble woke up and waddled to the food dish.

'Is it snack time already? Did you learn something from the show?' Sara asked the animals. The animals stopped their conversation and used their 'innocent' eyes with Sara. 'Something tells me you're plotting something.'

No, we're innocent, honest. Treats please. Big Bro thumped his tail on the floor until the treats were given.

See, I told you they wouldn't let us starve. That program was so lame. Barely touched the subject of scents. Didn't even see it from our perspective. Didn't even touch the smells in the air, body language, or anything. Slack, very slack, Strife chatted between mouthfuls of snacks.

Come on, it was a good start. You need a good baseline to work with. Next weeks' show should build on that. Big Bro slobbered on his chew stick.

Why do we have to let them know anything at all? Picasso challenged.

This is my final word. We must help our hoomans understand how we communicate. It's the only way. We must be tolerant of those not skilled in life and help them. Now, not another negative word or thought. We are so lucky to live in this house with this family. Be appreciative of what you have, keep yourselves positive. Big Bro directed.

That was a great snack! Did I miss anything? Trouble looked from one face to the other, oblivious to the conversation, inadvertently bursting the increasing tension.

Chapter 10: Skills and Abilities

The next day, after Sara and Tony went to work, last night's show was discussed further. All four animals began a heated discussion on the failings of the program.

Our working life goes back to the start of hooman existence. Hoomans would not exist if it wasn't for dogs, Big Bro began.

What about cats? We go back even further. Dogs were pack animals once. Cats were always dignified. You can see us with the kings and queens in Egypt, Strife retorted.

Yes, Strife, they had dogs also, but we're discussing last night's program about dogs. We, and cats, have been with hoomans for a very long time. We have always worked side by side with them in their everyday activities. Big Bro used his mediation skills to stop the building tension.

What? I don't work for hoomans – they work for me. See? They're off at work now, and I'm relaxing at home. Strife would not let it rest.

Yes, I understand your point, Strife. As I was saying, all of us are individuals. Each of us has our own special skills and abilities. For example, farm working dogs are specific breeds, such as Cassie, who is a Border Collie and helps to round up sheep. Or there is Rex, a Blue Heeler who helps round up cows while his person is on horseback. I'm a Kelpie and come from a long line of rounding things up on a farm. We take our cues from our eyesight, speed and our natural desire to keep things orderly. There is a range of dogs who help on a hunt, such as Retrievers or Setters, who help when catching birds. Bloodhounds, Beagles and similar dogs help with scents on the ground in finding lost or missing people. Beagles and Spaniels are also used as food or drug detection dogs as they can smell past hidden barriers to locate the offensive item. Alsatians, Dobermans and Rottweilers are also good in jobs of guarding and protecting. Other dogs help hoomans in different ways, such as Labradors, who help with vision impaired people. There are dogs who visit old people in nursing homes to bring cheer and get a pat. Big Bro expanded details from last night's program.

What about me? What job can I do? Picasso bounced.

You? Are you kidding? You're ... Strife started.

Strife, I'm warning you. Big Bro gave Strife a steely look. *Yes, even you have a specific skill set, Picasso. With your big ears, you can pick up strange noises from far away. Your greatest strength is to tell others about it.* Big Bro encouraged Picasso into identifying her own special skills.

Picasso looked perplexed about how to do this.

Humph, Big Bro motioned to Strife as she was about to snap a comment back. *You'll know – your instincts will kick in.* Big Bro nodded in a helpful manner to Picasso.

He means your mouth, Strife blurted out.

You mean a mouth can be used for something other than eating? Trouble questioned. Trouble's innocent logic shattered the tension with explosive laughter. Trouble, not understanding the joke, eventually succumbed to laughter as well, although she didn't know what she was laughing at. A truce was made.

Here, I'll show you how to work the remote. I'll toss it onto the ground, Strife calmly said.

Strife jumped on the chair and swatted the remote control off the side table. It dropped to the ground.

Flip it over, Trouble, Strife directed Trouble. Trouble showed how to flip it with her sharp claws.

See, this is what we excel at, Trouble said.

They all gathered around the remote control. Trouble pointed it towards the TV. *See this circle button on the top row? You need to press this first.* Strife joined the others on the floor.

What's a circle? Picasso asked.

It's the shape of the food bowl, Trouble declared.

Oh, I get it. Picasso nodded and returned to the remote-control demonstration.

Now, there are many buttons, and it can get confusing. See this big one on the side? One side moves the program to what you want, the one on the other side makes it loud. Don't use that one – it's too hurtful on our sensitive ears, Strife explained.

But our paws are too big. We'll hit too many buttons at once, Big Bro pointed out.

Ah-hah. Here's the trick. Use your nail on the side and gently press down. It's easier for me and Trouble as we can retract our claws and they're thinner than yours. Try anyway, Big Bro, Strife urged Big Bro.

Big Bro extended his paw towards the remote control and attempted to hit the button. He was clumsy at first, but eventually he hit the circle button and the TV sprung to life.

You've done it Big Bro! It's working. I hope I get to see the balls bouncing on the screen. Got to catch them one day. Strife raced toward the screen.

See this big button on the side? If we don't like what's showing, we can find something different. Trouble pressed the button a few times, until they found a noon-time movie with dogs and cats in it.

Oh hey. This is good, it has some outdoor animals to look at too. Trouble sat down to watch.

The others followed.

One final thing: make sure you turn it off by using the circle button at the end. Mum and Dad get spooked if they think they left it on, and of course they think nobody else could have turned it on. We'll keep this our little secret, Strife instructed.

The animals settled down to watch the movie with dogs and cats in it and marveled at the graciousness of animals enhancing hooman's lives. Hoomans should be grateful to have such wonderful, skilled pets in their lives.

Chapter 11: Life Perspectives

Not impressed seeing you chase that stupid ball all over the place. It seems you are doing all the work, while she just stands there and throws it to you, Picasso scolded Big Bro.

Nah, this is fun. Chasing the ball, rounding it up, bringing it back home. My eyes are my trade. It's inbuilt into me – I'm a Kelpie. My gene pool is designed to fetch, herd and corral back home. Big Bro's breath was heavy from all the running.

Well, I think it's silly – all that exercise and she does nothing, Picasso complained.

After several minutes of play, Big Bro overheated and, with the ball in his mouth, trotted to the dam. He entered up to his neck and panted hard, causing ripples to extend to the far sides. Picasso followed him to the top of the dam and waited for him.

Uh-un, not me, you won't get me in there. Looks too much like a bath, Picasso shook her head.

Nah umn im imuhs lumgd, Big Bro mumbled.

What? Take the ball out of your mouth. I didn't understand you, Picasso told Big Bro off.

Big Bro let go of the ball and it floated in front of him. *It is safe. I said, this is great. It cools you down, has a soft goo feeling between your toes and feels wonderful.*

Well, I'm not getting into it no matter how much you tempt me. It's the thought of getting wet all over and all my beautiful body smells getting replaced by something else. It took me such a long time rolling in things to get it just right, Picasso said.

The tennis ball had, unnoticeably, slowly sunk to the bottom of the dam. When Big Bro had cooled down enough, he looked around for his ball. *Have you seen the ball, Picasso?*

What? No, I don't care for balls, Picasso turned her head.

Then it must have sunk. I knew I shouldn't have punctured this one several times. It's under here somewhere, Big Bro said as his attention returned to the water. He prodded the bottom of the dam with his front legs to do a blind search for his ball. Bubbles rose from the bottom and burst on the surface. He has found it! Big Bro plunged his head right in and searched with his mouth. Bigger bubbles came to the surface and exploded. These ones must have come from Big Bro.

Horrified, Picasso was in disbelief as Big Bro had put his whole body underwater and not come up yet. Picasso raced to the water's edge and screamed, *Water: give me back my Big Bro, or I'll, I'll …*

Picasso had no time to finish her ultimatum as Big Bro surfaced with a splash, the tennis ball firmly in his mouth. He trotted out of the dam and shook the excess water off him, tennis ball in mouth. Picasso got sprayed by the water and high-tailed it to the top of the dam.

Eauw, yuk, dam water, yuk. Picasso was repulsed.

Ah wim telb to, Big Bro muffled from behind the ball.

What? Picasso asked.

Big Bro met Picasso at the top of the dam and laid down in the shade of the big tree. Putting the ball down and making sure it would not run away down the dam wall, he said, *Ah that feels better. It's amazing what is under the water, all sorts of interesting things.*

I thought the water had taken you away. You were in there a very long time. I thought I'd never see you again. The water is so murky, and I thought a monster got you. Did you see a monster? Did you see anything at all? Picasso fired questions at Big Bro.

I couldn't see much as I stirred the bottom up looking for my ball. There are no monsters in there, but lots of other things. You have to watch out for the nippers. They are small and can latch onto you with their strong sharp nips. I think Mum and the young children who visit call them yabbies. There are some small little fishes and sometimes I even get to see a tortoise! One day, I found at least eight tennis balls stuck in the mud. This was only when we had no rain and there was almost no water in the dam. This is probably where tennis balls are birthed. There are no monsters in the dam, Big Bro reassured Picasso.

Okay, but I still don't like water. How did you breathe under there? I saw huge bubbles coming up and thought you were in trouble. Picasso was concerned.

Bubbles come to the surface as there are living things in there. It is nice to find out what they are by going down and greeting them. You'll never know what you'll find. I'm hungry, lets go and get something to eat, Big Bro stated.

Big Bro, Picasso and the ball went back to the house. Sara had stopped playing when Big Bro went to the dam. Now, vacuuming noises could be heard.

I love getting vacuumed. It feels really good on your body. Fills you up with happy moods all over, Big Bro lovingly said.

Not me. I'm not stooping that low, Picasso disagreed with Big Bro.

Both dogs waited outside until Sara was finished with her chores. Picasso wanted to know more, and continually fired questions at her Big Bro.

So, there are living things under the water. How did you find out? Picasso questioned.

I've tested my theory many times and always come to the same conclusion. When it rains and a puddle forms, you will see living things bringing a bubble to the surface and pop. I've tried to dive and catch them, same as in the dam. You saw the bubbles rise from a living thing and burst on the surface, Big Bro explained.

Okay, I understand, Picasso said, not really understanding the full picture, but thought it would be better to say nothing. Picasso sighed and promised herself she would not go near water again, not in a dam or a puddle or anything else. She fell asleep dreaming of the many living things in a puddle or dam.

Chapter 12: Goodbyes and New Beginnings

The atmosphere in the house was chaotic. Household items were packed in boxes; bits of newspaper hid many delicate things that could break in transit. Pictures were taken off the walls. The stack of boxes increased in size in the back room while all the other rooms were being stripped bare. Walls, floors and blinds were scrubbed and cleaned. The shed and carport items were sorted, and some removed. The house cows left on a truck and the chickens were dropped off at Lara's house.

What's happening Big Bro? Everything's changing. I'm scared. Picasso quivered.

Nothing to be scared about. Mum and Dad have sold the house and we are moving. That's why they were painting the first night you came here. We are moving to 'town' with a nice big yard, Big Bro reassured Picasso.

But I don't want to move. I like it here now. I'm staying, Picasso whimpered.

If you stay, you will be by yourself. Everyone else is going. Come with us. You'll see – it should be good. Big Bro was ready for a change.

I don't want to be left alone, so I'll go. Can we leave the cats behind? Picasso suggested.

Big Bro shook his head and completed the final inspection of the house and yard to make sure everything was on track. Once his inspection was done, he saw Sara sitting at the back steps talking and cuddling with

Meatloaf, the Silky Terrier. Somehow, Big Bro knew Meatloaf had come to say goodbye and decided to give him and Sara space.

So, we won't see Meatloaf again? Picasso asked.

No, this is the last time, Big Bro sadly said.

But can't we come back for a visit? Picasso offered.

No. Meatloaf will go to eternal sleep soon. Can't you smell he is very sick and does not have much time? This is the very last time we will see him. Meatloaf and Mum need to say goodbye to each other. He is a special dog, very strong, fierce, loyal and kind. He helped me settle into this new house and area.

Tell me again how you came here and how you first met Meatloaf, Picasso urged.

Big Bro sighed heavily and commenced his story.

I was about two years old when I knew my life was about to change dramatically. There was me, and another dog, Ruby, an Alsatian. We knew one of us would have to go. Some people came out of a car, so I decided to show them my best quality – aloofness – as only Kelpies know best. I allowed my old family's baby to crawl all over me, pull my ears and tail, while I stared off into space, looking like the big deep philosopher that I am. I didn't know these people, but they seemed nice. I could smell kindness and care in them. After some discussion with my old owners, they picked me – I knew I was on a good wicket. They opened the back door to the car, and I jumped in without looking back. I was moving forward and upwards in my life.

I was immediately brought to a new home in the country and read the riot act by an Australian Silky called 'Meatloaf'. For three whole days he told me off, and that I was indeed very lucky to have landed here. He told me most of the history with this family and how special they are in his life. Meatloaf told me I have big boots to fill. I took this all in, and Meatloaf eventually became my best friend, with frequent visits, games and food. This new family also had an orange cat, which is very tolerant and accepting of me. She really is a good person too; I like looking out for her if she gets into any trouble. She told me she had been living on the streets after fleeing an abusive family before coming to this family, who treats her really nice. She deserves kindness and care. It's good to be needed and wanted as part of a family. We each have our own responsibilities: mine are to look after the property, make sure nothing attacks the chickens, look out for magpies, hawks, and eagles, watch the road, and make sure I get the cat's full approval.

I am fully aware that life is not a free ride, and that you have to work in order to be here. The lady and man work to get some money stuff to keep the roof over our heads and food in our belly, the cat attacks mice and rats, so they don't eat things they shouldn't. The chooks lay eggs and give us fertiliser for the gardens, and the cows cut the grass and also give us fertiliser. The lady said we need it all as the soil is so poor. I'm not sure about that, but it's good to keep busy and active. There are no silver serving platters here. Everybody must pull together and work as one as we all benefit. I am in my element and excel at many things. This is a good family to be placed with. Meatloaf would often visit and join in on many things.

'Thank you, Meatloaf, for the many years of company and care you showed me. I hope I've made some impact on your life.' Sara tenderly stroked the once glorious, shiny, silky coat of the Terrier.

I need to thank you, Sara, for your kindness, care and company. You always treated me well and included me in everything. Remember the time I could not see as my eye was all gummed up? I waited for you to fix me up. And the time there was that big brown snake by the fence? I barked to let you know and you helped to get the boys away. You pulled me out just in time or I would have been bitten and died. Or that time I got attacked and I had stiches in my side. You soothed me and cared for me. Although you are not my mom and I live with another family, which I love, you talk to me and spend quality time with me. I feel I could tell you anything and you would understand, Meatloaf said with adoration.

'Sometimes, Meatloaf, I feel as if I can truly communicate with you and understand every word you say. But sometimes, there are no words to say or explain things. Sometimes, it's just a feeling. I will miss you when you go. Thank you for sharing your life with me.' Sara gave the final pat, lingering on Meatloaf's head.

The two pals sat in silence for some time, each reflecting on their own memories of each other. Meatloaf gave one last look at Sara, then wandered over to Big Bro and Picasso. Unspoken words were exchanged; Big Bro lowered his head in respect. Meatloaf had no more emotional energy to say goodbye, but Big Bro understood. Meatloaf turned to go home; his entire body had lost vitality. Sadness eerily covered Sara, Big Bro, Picasso and the property.

The next morning, frenzied actions disrupted the entire house. A big van and two men arrived and put all the boxes, lounges, beds, and tables on the truck. Soon there was nothing left inside the house – an empty shell. The animals were tucked away in the cars (even the cats).

'The place looks so big when it's empty. There are ten years of memories holding up these walls,' Sara sighed.

'It's okay Sara, one part of our life has run its course. We're onto the next stage now. Bigger and better quality of life awaits us. You'll see, the next adventure is on our doorstep,' Tony reassured Sara.

'I suppose, but this is the first house we've owned. It will always be special – so many memories.' Sara reflected on the many activities and events the house has shared.

'C'mon now, time to go, or the moving van will be there before we will,' Tony urged Sara as he headed towards the car.

Sara had one more look around the house and vacant lounge. She sighed and locked the door behind her. The next adventure is impatient.

Meatloaf did not wake that morning.

Chapter 13: Changes and Adapting

Hey Big Bro, what's going on? How come they've kept us in the car? What's happening? Picasso whinged.

Don't worry, they're just unpacking all the big heavy stuff. It's safe for us here. We don't want to get underfoot, Big Bro reasoned.

No, let the little dog out, perhaps she'll get squashed and we won't have to deal with her any longer, Strife piped up.

What? No! Why are you so mean to me? Picasso shivered behind Big Bro.

That's enough, Strife. Picasso is part of the family now.

She's not part of mine. She's just a blow-in. She does not count.

Strife! How can you say that? We are all equal in this household. Each of us brings special things to the family. We should treat and give respect to all members. Big Bro raised his voice in protest.

Did someone say something? Is it time to eat? What are we doing here? Trouble finally woke up. Laughter burst throughout the car as Trouble always seemed to diffuse the situation. *Why is everyone laughing?*

It's okay Trouble, we were just talking about the move to the new house and not being trampled by all the moving boxes. Big Bro calmed his laughter.

Oh? Are we there yet? When do we get out? Do you think they remembered to pack our food bowls?

Yes, they would not forget about us, or our food. Strife settled down.

I wonder what new smells we will find. Okay, planning stations: Strife and Trouble, you check out the kitchen and bathroom areas first. I'll do a quick check of the lounge rooms and bedrooms, then we'll group back in the kitchen and compare notes, then we'll swap over. Big Bro organised the search.

What about me? What do I do? Picasso whimpered.

I know just what to do with you, I'll ... Strife began.

Strife, I'm warning you. You stick with me. I'll help you to tune your nose to the previous occupants, Big Bro reassured Picasso.

'That seems to be it, all in. Now, let me get my receipt book out, and calculate the actual time and kilometres, and Bob's your uncle.' The delivery man retrieved a clipboard from the cab of the truck and started scribbling something on the docket.

'That move went very quick. Now it's time to find a place to put everything. We might need to get some bookshelves or display cabinets, you know, to make it look more like a home.' Sara started to dream.

'Well, let's get this bill paid up and then we can rearrange all the big things before we start opening the boxes. It was a great idea you had labelling all the boxes. At least it will make things a bit easier for us,' Tony said.

'As soon as the removalists leave, we'll let the animals out to explore the house. I'm really concerned about having no fence up yet. Can you check to make sure they are coming tomorrow to do it? So many things to do when you move.' Sara ticked things off in her mind.

'Here you go, it didn't take us as long as what was originally quoted. I've knocked a hundred off the price.' Tony took the receipt with one hand, glanced at the figure and removed his wallet from his back pocket. He started peeling off the bills, counting up to the main figure.

'There you are. Thanks for doing this for us.' Tony handed the man the money for the job. They said goodbye and the man hoisted himself into the cabin of the truck, kicked over the ignition and drove away in a big cloud of black diesel smoke.

What's that paper-like stuff they are exchanging? Picasso asked Big Bro.

It's called money, stupid. It's what they bargain for jobs with. See, the delivery man does something, and gives Dad gives a piece of paper for it. In return, he gets a whole bunch of smaller paper bits back. Doing this sort of stuff seems to work for them. I don't understand why they have to exchange bits of paper, but they would be lost without it. I sometimes think they need bits of paper to line their own kitty litter box, Strife reasoned.

'Why don't we let the animals out of the car, and into the house? They must be going mad in there with all the movement. The sooner they get settled into the house, the better,' Sara directed Tony.

'Let's hope they don't go for the main road – I'd hate it if we lost them as soon as we arrive,' Tony said with concern.

Tony and Sara opened the car doors and the animals leapt out and started sniffing the ground and the air, having their first look at their new environment. They felt the grass and the gravel footpath by the house and started sniffing the outside. Both dogs marked their new area in style.

Ugh, so uncouth, Big Bro. No privacy here at all, Strife replied.

Wow. There are so many new smells here. So much has happened. There's been all sorts of everything here at some point in time, Big Bro excitedly said.

Big Bro let his nose lead him to many spots. Picasso tried to keep up, but there were just too many ways to turn before a new smell turned up.

It took me so long to get the smell of the last place. It will take me forever to get the hang of this place, Picasso admitted.

Well, we could always get the delivery truck to bring you back. I'm sure nobody will miss you, Strife spat.

What? Are we staying or are we going? I thought we were going to check out the kitchen. Let's go. Trouble started for the door.

Strife, you need to settle down and not pick on Picasso so much. Will you ever learn? Big Bro was exasperated.

I did not ask for her, she just showed up. She has a long way to go to prove herself.

Keep her out of my way, Big Bro, Strife retaliated.

Can we keep our attitudes to ourselves? We are starting afresh – a new slate, so mind your tongue. Big Bro trotted through the door after Trouble.

'Sometimes, I think this lot talk amongst themselves. I have a sneaky suspicion they are talking about us,' Sara commented as all four animals headed for the house.

'Don't be silly, Sara. Animals can't talk – you're just tired and excited about the move. C'mon, let's get in and unpacked.' Tony led the way. Sara continued to scrutinise the animals.

Sara and Tony entered the lounge area and re-positioned the lounges and side tables to suit the TV. Tony hooked up the TV aerial and started to tune it in with the remote control. They both moved to the different areas of the house, adjusting the chairs, tables, beds and wardrobes. Big Bro and Picasso reviewed each room. The old carpet held a variety of smells of life that they tried to interpret each area. The cats were inspecting every inch of the kitchen and were disappointed to find only a big bowl of water down.

I guess this is where we will eat. Not nice – feels too open. Do you suppose we'll all eat here, in the same place? Strife questioned her sister.

It is a big room – much bigger than the last place. Hey! Do you think we'll have bigger plates? We've got enough room for them here, trilled Trouble.

Somehow, I don't think so. C'mon, let's look some more. There are certainly some funky smells going on in here. Something smelly seems to be coming straight through the wall. Come here and smell this area. Strife pointed to a section of the wall.

Yeah. I see what you mean. It's big, but it also seems to have been there a long time. The scent is still there, Trouble commented.

The cats continued to sniff everywhere in the kitchen, and then headed into the laundry and bathroom areas for a quick look and sniff. Soon, Big Bro and Picasso arrived in the kitchen area and met Trouble and Strife coming back from the bathroom.

Wow – there certainly is much going on in here. Let's swap areas and then we can compare notes, Big Bro said to the cats. After several minutes, all four pets gathered in the kitchen to exchange information.

So much has happened in here. So much information to process, Strife started.

It seems like years and years all built up on top of each other, Trouble added.

I wonder how old this house is. It seemed like we could have retraced to the original smells of the house, Big Bro commented.

Could you smell all the animals that have been here? Strife said.

And the food that has been spilt on the carpet? Trouble pointed out.

And what about the front room – smells like car oil to me, Big Bro stated.

I wonder why people would bring a car into that small front room? Strife wondered.

I think it leads to the door – did you see it? I could smell the outside from there. Perhaps they could drive it through? Picasso imagined.

Nah, it would never fit. Cars are big, it wouldn't fit through the doorway, Big Bro deduced.

Would a small car fit? Picasso added.

No such thing as a small car that size, Strife stated.

But what if it was like a car, but smaller, much smaller. What about a motorcycle. You know the ones that bring the mail to the mailbox? It could have been one like that. Big Bro tempted the others' imaginations.

Yeah, it could have. Did you check out the bathroom? How weird, Trouble quizzed.

A big space in the corner with nothing in it. I wonder why it is done like that? Big Bro questioned.

I could smell traces of metals – soft, sweet ones. And heat. Something was boiling in that area, Strife mentioned.

The animals chatted for a long time before they all fell silent, lost in their own thoughts. Dreams of weird things making the smells invaded their nap time.

Sara and Tony had completed setting up a few rooms and had unpacked some of the boxes marked 'clothes.' Sara decided to turn her attention to the kitchen before she got too carried away with the boxes. All the animals were spread out on the kitchen floor. This was a good time to start getting this room in order. She began to wipe down the kitchen counters, shelves and drawers before finding a place to put all the plates and cups and cutlery.

Tony thought this was a good time to check on the fence installers and look at any other outside work that needed to be done. This yard was a blank canvas ready for Tony to create an awesome place. Both Sara and Tony stepped around the sleeping animals to do their own chores. The animals stirred slightly, but then went back to sleep. Sara smiled at the peaceful pets resting.

Chapter 14: The Art of Learning

The new place would take some time to get used to: new smells, layout, and spaces. Everything needed to be readjusted. Luckily, food arrived at approximately the same time as in their other place and was very much welcomed. As predicted, the animals all lined up against the long wall and had their own spaces to eat.

The next day, two workmen arrived, creating much noise, clatter and mess. A new wooden fence was put up from the front corner of the house to the side fence. The other side of the house was matched with the same wooden fence, but a swinging gate was also installed across the driveway. This ensured the animals would be safe in the large back yard. When the gate was up, and the workmen had gone for the day, Big Bro, Picasso, Strife and Trouble were allowed out the back to explore the yard.

It was very bland, lots of smells, but also devoid of interesting things. There was a dilapidated garage that seemed it would fall down in a slight breeze and a palm tree that shed little orange seed nuts – their rotting pits could be smelt in the thick grass below. There were a few trees scattered down the back-fence line, and that was it. The rest was just grass, but the smells still lingered in the ground. The yard was big enough to keep inquisitive animals occupied – even under the house presented amazing finds.

The noise from outside the fence and on the road was constant: cars, trucks, buses and pedestrians were going up and down all day long.

I thought they were putting us in prison, with all these bars of wood keeping us in. Picasso was worried.

This is here to protect us from the outside. It would be too easy to wander into the pathway of the busy road. We don't want to get hurt from any of those big cars or trucks, do we? Big Bro said.

I suppose not; it seems very scary out there. Picasso stuck close to Big Bro.

Are you sure? You could always try to play with them – see how far you get, Strife urged.

Strife! Don't tease Picasso. Stop it now, Big Bro scolded. Strife put her nose in the air and sauntered towards the back door.

'Ah, here you are, I've got a collar for you to wear. Now you're living in town, you must wear one of these.' Sara came towards Picasso with something in her hands.

Not me, this is not good, I'm out of here, Picasso ran away from Sara.

Big Bro chuckled as he watched Sara chase after Picasso in the back yard with the collar in her hands. Eventually, Sara brought out some food to trick Picasso and snuck up on her and clipped the collar on. Picasso squealed like a suckling pig and tried to get it off.

Get it off of me, I'm dying, I'm possessed, I'm being poisoned by this terrible thing. Help, Big Bro, help, Picasso cried.

Silly dog, we all wear collars. Strife became intolerant of Picasso's drama queen antics.

Picasso, it's okay. It doesn't hurt. It's okay to wear a collar. It's really fashionable and handy. Settle down, Big Bro reassured Picasso.

No. I. Won't. I am not a slave. I am not wearing a collar. I am not having this. I am not going to be branded to a household or domestication. I want to be free. This is too degrading. Get it off of me. If the mighty dog entity in the sky wanted me to wear a collar, She would have given me one at birth. This is not on – I won't stand for it, Picasso complained.

Picasso continued to squirm and tried to get it off. Picasso cried and kicked and carried on for many hours. Sara kept shaking her head and hoped the puppy would soon get used to the collar. Sara felt for the distress Picasso was putting herself under.

'I wish you could settle her down, Big Bro. It really doesn't hurt if you wear a collar, and it's the law. All companion animals must wear a collar, have an ID badge with name and contact phone number, and have a microchip. We need these things in case you get lost. Please make her understand,' Sara pleaded with Big Bro.

Hey, Picasso, it's okay wearing a collar – all fashionable pets wear one. It's okay, settle down, Big Bro calmly said.

Not having it ... I'm getting it off. Picasso continued to struggle with the collar.

After several more days, almost all the fight was gone from Picasso. She soon became resigned to wearing this degrading thing. It honed her determination and drive of what is not acceptable and what is. In the meantime, Picasso swore she would not trust Sara – how could she do this to her? What else is she going to do to her?

That something else soon arrived in the form of a long strip of mesh with a hook on one end that could be attached to the collar. This allowed Picasso to be walked on a lead, which was controlled by Tony or Sara. Big Bro readily joined in as it meant going out and seeing the new neighbourhood, meeting new people and smells. Picasso had other ideas. She kicked and carried on for the longest time and tried to squirm her way out of it. Somehow, she would often do it so well that she escaped from the confines of the collar and lead. It was then very interesting to see Sara chase after a black blur running as far away as she could. This created no end of stress for Sara and Picasso.

'I can't handle this anymore, Tony. Picasso is so stressed, and so am I. This collar and lead are not working. I've got to try something different. I'll look at the pet shop on my way home from work tomorrow,' Sara sighed.

'Whatever you find, I hope it does the trick. Nothing seems to be working with Picasso,' Tony concluded.

See, I told you she does not belong here – send her back Big Bro, Strife stated.

Strife, no more. She does belong with this family. She's just having a difficult time adjusting. Sometimes this happens. We need to be kind and patient with her. We have no idea what has happened to her to act like this. Perhaps she was almost strangled with something when she was with her birth family. She's stressed, so it's up to all of us to encourage peace into her world, Big Bro pleaded.

Strife took this into consideration. We don't always know how, what, or why others do things the way they do. Strife's ability to adjust must be quicker than Picasso's. She'll give her time to settle – but not too much longer. Strife always hated whingers.

The next evening, Sara presented Picasso with a soft, red leather strap thing, and, holding it up, excitedly exclaimed, 'Hopefully, this will work, Picasso.' Sara put Picasso's head through one hole and started on a leg before Picasso realised what it was. She started twisting and turning to exit herself from the red leather strap thing.

No, this is no good. Something is seriously wrong with this thing. I thought it was a toy, but I can smell no good on it. Help me, Big Bro, help me. Picasso panicked.

A struggle began as Sara was trying to get the harness on Picasso, Picasso trying to get the harness off. Every time Sara almost got it clipped at Picasso's back, Picasso would squirm around, and it would half fall off her. Sara and Picasso and the red harness were in a fierce battle: just who would win was not evident. After several minutes, and an attempt to flee from Picasso, Sara finally won and got the red harness snapped onto Picasso. Picasso squirmed and wriggled and pushed and pulled with all her might to get the harness off. No matter what she did, it would not budge. Sara made herself a cup of tea and sat down in the lounge.

'I didn't think it would be so hard, Picasso. Why can't you be like the others?' Sara gave a heavy sigh.

Picasso continued to wriggle, acting up as if she were mortally wounded, and dragging herself from one area of the house to the other, rubbing the side of her body on the carpet in hopes this would pull it off.

I'm dying with this thing on me, help me get it off. I can't breathe, I can't walk. Have mercy on me. Picasso's behaviours were becoming boring.

For such a small dog, you sure do carry a big dramatic role. Perhaps you could get an Oscar for acting up? Strife sneered.

Tony walked in the door to the commotion. 'What's this? A harness. What a great idea – and it fits too.'

'I had to get a get a cat one as they didn't have a small enough one for Picasso. I thought the red would look good against her shiny black fur.' Sara perked up a bit.

Hahaha. Did you hear that? Picasso's got a cat harness on. Picasso's got a cat harness, Strife chanted.

Strife, that's enough. Poor Picasso is feeling bad enough already. Big Bro stepped in.

Yeah, but it is funny. Hey, Trouble, look. Picasso has a cat harness on, and we should be kind to her in her stress. Strife tried to stop herself from chuckling.

A cat harness? I never knew there was such an invention. It's a miniature one, isn't it? Trouble inspected Picasso in the harness.

No, it's normal size for cats. I don't think it would fit you either. You're too big for it. Strife tried hard not to laugh.

I'm not big, I'm normal size. I just happen to have thick fur. I'm heading for a snack. Trouble sauntered towards the kitchen.

'I plan to have Picasso wear this for short periods of time, until she gets used to it. Hopefully this won't take long and will be less distressing to her.' Sara reflected on the pet shop assistants' instructions.

Both Sara and Tony took turns in putting the harness on and off Picasso. With time, she got used to wearing it and the feel of it under her armpits, throat and back. Next, Sara hooked up the lead to the back 'D' clips. This was almost too much to bear, and Picasso felt the weight and drag of the lead. Once again Picasso squirmed, wriggled and carried on like she was being mortally wounded with the lead.

From this stage, Sara and Tony took Big Bro and Picasso out for a walk. Big Bro excited in the front on his lead as he got to see the neighbours and the smells from the last time. Picasso, once again, dragged behind.

C'mon, Picasso, keep up. You're missing all the good smells from way behind there, Big Bro called out and urged Picasso on.

Not happy at all. I've got to wear the harness which brings me out in huge welts, and now I've got to drag a long rope thing behind me. It trips me up and it gets caught on things. This is not fair, Picasso complained.

The harness does not bring you out in welts. Stop exaggerating. And if you keep up, Sara will hold the other end of the leash and it will be easier to walk. C'mon, try, Big Bro explained.

It feels like welts – all the time. I don't want to do this, Picasso grumbled.

Ah hah. It's because you are stubborn, is that it? Stop being so. You're making everyone upset – especially yourself. Get off your high horse, Big Bro retorted.

'Are you ready to learn to walk properly, Picasso?' Sara bent down to catch the end of the lead.

Did you hear her talk to me that way, Big Bro? I don't like to be told off in that way, and I'm not on a horse, Picasso said indignantly.

Just do what I do. If you give it a chance, you'll find out that it is so much better when you have fun and don't argue all the time. Arguing makes you sad and brings you down. There is no time in life to be sad like this. Enjoy the walk with me, Tony and Sara. Big Bro continued to sniff the pathway, trees and fences.

I feel I've been tricked. I don't want to conform; I want to do my own thing. Picasso was resigned to following Big Bro, Tony and Sara.

We have to conform on the outside, because if we don't the ranger will come by and take us away. We'll be locked up far away from our family. It's not a good place to be. This makes sure that we and other community members are safe and secure at all times. Besides, it's the law to be fine upstanding citizens, Big Bro explained more.

I still hate it, but I suppose I have no choice, Picasso grumbled and allowed Sara to pick up the end of the lead and walk.

Chapter 15: Behaviours and Personalities

'There's a harassment case happening at work now. I'm not sure where or how it started, but it's turning nasty. The whole office is feeling the tension,' Sara said one night to Tony.

'What's happening? Who is it with?' Tony's moustache twitched.

'I think it's between Cheryl and Mick,' Sara admitted.

'That Mick thinks he's a ladies' man, but he's too sleazy,' Tony dismissed.

'Their paths should not normally pass, but I think they keep bumping into each other at unexpected times. Cheryl has come back to her desk pretty shaken many times and won't talk about what's bothering her. I think it's been going on for quite a while,' Sara explained more.

'What's going to happen? Does anybody know what really went on?' Tony asked with concern.

'I think they're trying to sort it out, but I also think WorkCover has been involved as well,' Sara said.

'WorkCover? Don't they usually deal with accidents at work?' Tony quizzed.

'I think this must be pretty big if they are involved. They also cover many other things. We're not union represented, so I suppose WorkCover or the Anti-Discrimination board looks after things.' Sara shrugged.

'Sounds like big business. Hope it gets sorted out.' Tony returned to the TV.

What does harassing mean? Picasso asked.

Harassing means doing something that annoys another and keep doing it even though they've been told to stop, Big Bro explained.

So why do they keep doing it? Picasso asked.

I'm not fully sure, but I think they might have something loose and their respect meter is off-kilter. Harassing and bullying can sometimes go hand in hand, Big Bro reasoned.

What's bullying? I've seen a Bully Ant, is it something like that? Picasso asked again.

Bullying is stronger than harassing. Bullying can have bad effects on people: too ill to work, destroying their self-esteem and self-worth, making their lives miserable. Big Bro sighed.

Why do they do it? Picasso wanted more information.

These people have no love in their bodies, have a large jealous streak in them and want to make everyone else just as miserable as they are. Don't fall for their rubbish, stay away from them. They are no good to anyone. Big Bro tried to give simple, practical advice.

So how do we stop them doing it? Picasso said.

Bullies are like this for special reasons. Maybe they are jealous of you or what you have, maybe they come from a broken home and can't get any love there, maybe they don't know how to mix or communicate, maybe they themselves are being bullied and harassed and do this to others to make themselves feel good. There could be any number of reasons, Big Bro said.

It seems a deeper problem than first thought. Picasso mimics Big Bro's thoughts.

Finding out why they are doing this is one of the steps in finding out how to fix this. By understanding from their point of view, we might start to understand this bad behaviour, Big Bro continued.

But what if they're picking on you and have started a fight. Do I stay and fight back? Picasso questioned.

You can sense when there is aggression starting. Stay away from aggression – it will tear you up from the inside. Tell them to stop as you don't want this sort of behaviour, and leave, Big Bro stated.

But what if it keeps going on? Picasso had more questions.

Most of the time they will back off, but if they don't, find a mature person to help you on the way, Big Bro offered.

Like you? Picasso stated.

Yes, like me or any other responsible person. They must hear you and your story and try to help you. Sometimes, I think the bullies just want to get a reaction. If you ignore them, then they might move on and leave you alone, Big Bro stated.

But if they try it on someone else, isn't that just as bad? Picasso continued.

Yes, it is. The bully needs help to sort out their feelings, emotions and behaviours. Big Bro sighed.

Who can help? Picasso was never short of questions.

People at school, work, in the community, on the internet, people like Mum or Dad who have respectable jobs. Big Bro had started to feel tired.

Does this also apply to Strife and Trouble? Well, mainly Strife. Why does she hate me so much? Why does she pick on me all the time? I don't like it, Picasso complained.

I've told her not to, Big Bro answered.

But Strife is still doing it. Why does she do it? Picasso wanted an answer.

I guess she's jealous of having to share the house, family and me with someone else. She's older than you are, so she might be very cranky towards younger, more energetic ones. I'll have another talk with her. Big Bro closed his eyes and rested

'Well, it's really hit the fan today. Industry bosses were waiting for the office to open and called in all the managers and supervisors for a meeting. They then called in Cheryl and spoke to Mick privately. Apparently, there were some nasty surprises said at the meeting,' Sara reported.

'How do you know all this? Were you eavesdropping?' Tony accused.

'Nah, the office grapevine let us know. It doesn't take much to put two and two together, big trouble,' Sara replied.

'What's going to happen?' Tony asked.

'Not sure, we'll wait and see. I don't think anyone knew how bad it was for Cheryl. Why can't people respect each other? It makes you wonder what values they were brought up on. I've had a long chat with one of the members, and they told me the process – seems fascinating. I kept asking and asking without being too insensitive – mainly about the process and the work they do. I also asked if there was some way we could have stopped this and how to stop this happening in the future, and she gave me some really good information.' Sara beamed and shook her head and her spiky brown hair competed in the shake.

'You're not sticking your nose in again, are you? I guess some people think they're the best and can do nothing wrong. Mick's got a huge chip on his shoulder; I don't think he'll change,' Tony continued.

'His parents seem okay. I wonder what happened to him to make him act this way?' Sara wondered.

'Don't be fooled. You don't know what happens behind closed doors. They may seem fine on the surface, but put a few beers into his old man, and he becomes verbally nasty, and his true colours come out,' Tony warned.

'You'd never guess. I suppose we tend to take things at face value. But I suppose you never really know someone until you walk around in their shoes,' Sara quoted from one of her favourite books.

I guess it takes all sorts to make the world go around, Picasso wondered.

Yes, Little One, it does take all sorts. These differences also enrich our lives – it would be very boring if everyone was the same. We need variety to keep life interesting. But keep all the good supportive and positive people in your life – we don't need the negative ones, Big Bro said.

Is variety only good for people? Picasso asked.

Variety is good in all things: hoomans, dogs, cats, trees, houses, even the food places. There's variety there too. We all get a chance to choose the things we want or like better than the other. It gives us power in our own lives to be able to make a good decision by viewing other options. Remember, there never is just one way to do things, look at the variety. Big Bro hummed.

Chapter 16: I've Got Bling

'It was such an ordeal with Picasso's collar, harness and lead that I never want to go through that again,' Sara discussed with Tony over the evening meal.

'It needs to be done. We need to protect our animals from harm. We need to do the right thing, or the ranger will take them away,' Tony chimed in.

What? They'll take you away? Why didn't you say so? I'll help you to keep the harness off – run free little dog. Strife is elated.

Strife – she is just getting there. Leave it alone – not another word from you. You will not harass or bully her anymore, Big Bro warned.

'There're other things we need to do too. Like registering her with council,' Sara mentioned.

'And microchipping. I think that needs to be done first so they can register the number and get her de-sexed,' Tony added.

'Well, I guess that means booking her into the V-E-T. We might as well get the whole thing done while she's there. She's not a pure breed, we won't be breeding her, and we don't want any unexpected puppies, so she'll have to go in for the full service. I'll phone tomorrow to see when they can do her,' Sara stated.

What are they talking about, Big Bro? I've got a strange feeling they're talking about me, and it doesn't sound too good from here. Picasso was worried.

Don't worry, every dog and cat need to be microchipped, just in case we get lost. The rangers can easily find out our details and bring us home again. It's a responsible thing to do, Big Bro explained.

What's a microchip? Does it taste nice? Picasso asked.

Yeah, does it? I'd like one. Trouble woke up and joined the conversation.

No, Trouble, remember? We both got one done when we were kittens. It's a little thing that's under our skin on our back, Strife explained.

I've got one too. It doesn't hurt at all, and you don't even realise you have it there, Big Bro said.

Well, okay. Maybe. But it still doesn't feel right to me. I think something more is up. Picasso headed off to sleep, her mind racing with thoughts of inserting horrible things under her skin at the back. Perhaps they'll even insert the harness under there?

The next day, Sara arranged a time for Picasso to get her microchip and special fixing.

Tell me again what this microchip thing is. And what was Sara saying about special fixing? I'm still not sure on this, Picasso wondered.

A microchip is a very small thing that when scanned, a long number comes up and they can trace you to your family, Big Bro explained.

Yeah, I know that, but what exactly is a microchip? Picasso said.

It is small, shiny and looks very expensive and elegant. Have you seen the ring on Mum's finger? It looks like that. All shiny and sparkly. I think Mum calls it her 'diamonde.' This is what I, Trouble and Strife have. And you will have one too. You won't be able to feel it, but you'll always know you're special as you will have this with you always, Big Bro gushed.

I suppose. Mum's diamonde is pretty. It will be nice for me to have one of my very own, Picasso admitted.

That's the ticket. Big Bro beamed.

Big Bro had finally eased the situation. There is always another way to explain things; words can be interchanged to suit the situation. He dared not tell Picasso of the other 'special fixing' that will happen. He clearly remembered his time: the indignation of his body parts removed, the secret room at the back of the V-E-T's where it happened, being drugged and knocked out, having to wear a bucket on his head for a week. No, best not to tell Picasso of what will happen. She's too stressed at this point. Let her find out herself when the time comes.

'Hey, Picasso, you have an appointment in three days' time. We'll get you all fixed up: microchipping, register with council, and a few other things too. I'm also going to get your teeth looked at as you look like a shark. Your baby teeth are competing with your adult teeth, or is it the other way around? Anyway, you're all set to get everything working. I'll even get you something special.' Sara grabbed her car keys and bounced out of the house.

Later that evening, Sara presented Picasso with a new collar. It was black with beautiful diamonds all around it. Picasso was hesitant at first, but the look of all the shiny, sparkly diamonds was enticing.

See Picasso, these are diamondes, just like Mum has on her finger, just like I have on my back. What a beautiful gift. Big Bro was enthusiastic.

Picasso looked to Sara, then Big Bro, and back to the diamond.

'Here Picasso. I thought it would be nice to show you off in a beautiful necklace. I saw this one the other day and thought this would be perfect for you. No ugly collars for you. Such a beautiful one with little bling diamonds for you. A real stunner you'll be. Here, try it on!' Sara held out the necklace for Picasso to sniff.

A necklace? Full of diamondes? Just for me? Did you hear her, Big Bro? No collars for me. A real necklace. Wow! Picasso excitedly gushed.

Picasso let Sara take off the old collar and replace it with her new, beautiful necklace.

I've got bling and diamondes now. Look at me. I must be so special. Picasso pranced.

You are special. You look very beautiful, Big Bro crooned.

'I guess it's all in the way you present things. We've had such a hard time with her adjusting to things. It's been really hard on all of us. So, I thought if I called things by different names, maybe she would accept things more readily. I think it worked. Look at her now, she's feeling so great,' Sara discussed with Tony that night.

'It'll be good for her to go into her operation feeling great. Imagine if she was still digging her heels in? How stressful would it be then? It's great to see her feeling good. But I hope it lasts throughout her operation, it'll be a big shock to her.' Tony was concerned.

'We can adapt our ways to make things worthwhile. Our behaviours can be easily managed just by adjusting our words. I learnt this through the Cheryl and Mick saga,' Sara reasoned.

A few days later, Sara picked Picasso up and said goodbye to the rest of the animals.

See ya later. I'm going for my diamonde, Picasso excitedly yapped.

She doesn't fully know, does she? Strife was concerned.

No, she doesn't know. I thought it would best for her. She gets stressed at such little things. I thought it would be kinder to do it this way, Big Bro admitted.

I remember when I had the operation, and how I felt. I wouldn't wish this on anyone, Strife reflected.

Yeah, it took me a long time to come good, didn't it? I didn't want to do anything for days, Trouble piped up.

I had to wear a bucket on my head for a week – how embarrassing. All the neighbours were laughing and teasing me. It was horrible. Big Bro shivered in remembrance.

I solemnly swear I will turn over a new leaf, as of now. No more teasing the little dog. Strife glanced towards Big Bro and got a nod of approval.

Poor little dog. I'm glad Sara gave her that necklace. It would have made her happy, Trouble pondered.

Okay, let's do everything we can to make her feel better when she comes home, Big Bro directed, and both cats agreed.

Picasso did not arrive home that night but came home the day after. Feeling very sorry for herself, she did not greet anyone, but went straight for her basket and closed her eyes and shivered.

Putting the blanket over her, Sara told Tony all the news from the vet.

'She bit several of them at the clinic. They were going to brand her a vicious dog. I'm not a hundred percent sure, but I think they took it out on her when she went under. They extracted the baby teeth that were intruding on her adult teeth, but several of them broke. They had to dig to get all the bits out. They did this by cutting into her gums. Poor little dog – so distressing. I don't know how much they know when they're under, but it seems she had a hard time. Her operation went well when she was spayed, so that was fine, I suppose. Poor little one, she's had a tough time.' Sara was sullen.

'How could this happen? They never told us anything yesterday when we were going to pick her up. They just said she's still coming around and needs a night to recuperate. What about the microchip? And the paperwork? Is it all in, all okay?' Tony questioned.

'That's the other big story. They decided to put the microchip in before the operation. Apparently, she twisted and squirmed and wriggled and fought like a trouper. This is when she started biting the staff. They made several attempts before they eventually got it in, but she broke loose and wriggled it further down her back. It's supposed to show up behind her shoulder blades, but she made it move further down and on her right side. I'm appalled that they put her through so much stress. I warned them that she can become very upset, but obviously they didn't listen. They tried and tried to get a muzzle on her for it. Can you imagine how she reacted to this? Remember getting her to wear a collar and harness? When I picked her up and questioned details, they told me everything. I asked them: 'Don't you think it would have been better to put the microchip in while she was under to stop all the stress?' They just shrugged. I'm not impressed, and I think I will have to find another vet,' Sara commented.

'Well, she's gone through an ordeal, let her rest for a few days. I'm sure she'll bounce back soon,' Tony hoped.

Big Bro, Trouble and Strife all lined up in front of Picasso's bed as a mark of respect.

It was never that bad with me, Big Bro said.

Nor me, in and out in a day, Trouble chimed in.

Poor little dog. How do we help her? Strife said with remorse.

Strife, that is the kindest thing you have said. We'll just take our cues from Picasso. I'll save her the best bits in food – that might help, Big Bro offered.

Give up some of my food? What if I starve? Trouble glanced at the sombre faces looking back at her. *Okay, she can have some of my food.*

I wonder if hoomans go through the same thing? It would serve them right to know how it feels to be treated like this. Being poked and prodded by a stranger, microchipped and even getting something up their behinds to check their temperature. They're quite primitive, aren't they? Strife reflected.

Thank you, Trouble and Strife. Yes, I'm sure hoomans do similar things as we go through. Now, let Picasso rest. I'll stand guard. Big Bro took his position beside her basket while the cats moved away.

Chapter 17: Blended Families

The experience of Picasso's V-E-T visit helped to bond all the animals in the household. It's amazing how tragedy is a magnet for love, caring and sharing. It's also our nature to help someone who is doing it tough. It's our responsibility to ensure as many of the members of the community are safe and well.

Although Trouble and Strife had vowed to be kinder to Picasso, and even shared some of their food, Picasso's trust had been shattered. She stayed close to Big Bro and listened as he prattled about the ways of the world.

Everything in the world is called something. It gets confusing if we say thing, this or that all the time. Therefore, placing names on things clarifies what you are talking about and gives meaning to life. For example, if we do not have a name, how can we know who anybody or anything is? If someone calls out, 'Hey you,' then a whole group of hoomans or animals will turn to see who you mean. Hence, having names is essential in life, Big Bro chattered.

I understand, but I still don't want to come when I'm called. It might mean another visit to the V-E-T. I don't want to ever go back there. I'm still suffering nightmares from that place and what I had to go through. Perhaps I can pretend not to hear them calling me? Picasso complained.

I can only imagine what traumas you went through. It's over now and I'm sure you will never have to go through that again. I heard them talking about never sending you back to that particular place ever again. As to not answering when they call you, it will do you well to answer. The reason they call could be varied, like a ride in the car, a walk, a treat, food, a cuddle or a pat. It will do you good to follow their instructions. Bad things can happen if you don't behave. Remember I told you about the Ranger? You don't want to be caught by him, do you? You'll end up in a small cage like cell. The community would not approve. I urge you to reconsider and answer when called. It's plain good manners, Big Bro explained.

Fine, I'll try, but I'm still very scared of going back to that place. I never want to go there again. How do you know they won't trick me?

I'm sure of it, you heard them say it too, I believe in them. We share our lives with hoomans, and they share theirs with us. We understand them more than they understand us. As I was saying, they use names to describe many things such as other people, things, objects, animals, and so forth. We know these names and react appropriately. The love and sharing we have with our hooman family make us a part of their lives. This is why I call Sara and Tony Mum and Dad, you know, endearing, Big Bro said.

What's endearing again? Picasso quizzed. *I forgot.*

Endearing is when you care very much for someone and even grow to love them. Your world revolves around them, and you would do anything for them. Our closest hoomans are therefore also called Mum and Dad. Big Bro oozed love.

No way, I'm not calling them that. I had a mum and dad – although I can't seem to remember them much now, Picasso admitted. Picasso squeezed her eyes shut, trying to remember their smell, look, touch, and her mother's tongue and body. Chuckling, Big Bro continued with Picasso.

I know our mum is not our birth mother, but a mum can also do many different things. A mum looks after and cares for us, they cook and clean, fix up flea problems and worm problems, give us medicine when we are ill, listen to us and sometimes watch TV or read a book with us. They can go for a walk or a drive, a swim or play tennis with us. Birth mothers are always special, for if it was not for them, we would not be here. Mothers come in all shapes and sizes; they have different personalities and provide us with the best of everything. Each household is different, so each mum is different. This also goes for dads as well. Dads are good, and they have their role to play as well. They can do most things mums can do. Big Bro allowed these ideals wash over Picasso before he continued again.

The same goes for everyone we live with. Strife and Trouble are not my biological kittens, but I love them all the same. There is more to life than your gene pool. There is no one definition for family; families come in all shapes and sizes. Tolerance comes in all shapes and forms. For example, some hoomans often say, 'Dogs, cats and birds do not mix,' but we do. I'm a dog, Trouble and Strife are cats, and we used to have a canary in a cage. We all live under the same roof; we all share the same space, Big Bro stated.

So, I'm supposed to love the cats? And care for them too? Picasso questioned.

Yes, they are part of this family. This means accepting, tolerating, compromising, sharing. We are all different; we all have our own personalities, strengths and weaknesses. We need to understand these things and learn to get along with others. Family comes in any shape or size. Sometimes, there are two mums or two dads, sometimes there is a grandparent, sometimes there is an aunty or uncle, sometimes there are several unrelated family members, or sometimes we are placed in foster families. A family is a place where you are loved, cared for and a safe place to be. Family is what you make it to be, Big Bro continued.

But I get along with you very well, so I stick by you all the time. Strife always picks on me, and Trouble is like a cannonball when it comes to eating time. I've learned to give the cats a wide berth, Picasso said.

Have you noticed that Strife is not bothering you as much? And that Trouble is sharing some of her food? They've become more tolerant and accepting of you, Big Bro pointed out.

Yeah, I had noticed it. How come? Picasso quizzed.

Well, we've all realised your strengths and natural tendencies, and we are adapting our interactions with you. It seems to be working. Big Bro would not let Picasso know the whole truth.

Strength and tendons? Exactly what does that mean? Picasso wanted to know more.

It's strengths and natural tendencies. This is how each of us tackle things in our lives. It's who we are: our likes, dislikes, and the way we do things. This is a mixture of our breeds, our upbringing, and intellectual stimulation. Big Bro puffed his chest out and showed off his natural Kelpie aloofness.

So who am I? What am I? Where do I fit in? How do I know who I am? Picasso asked.

You have a good head start with your breed. Just follow your instincts – you'll know the right path to take. Big Bro smiled.

Both dogs lay down in the back yard for a well-deserved snooze, Big Bro dreaming of the joys of a mixed family, Picasso wondering who she really is.

Chapter 18: i, Chihuahua

'Okay, time for our walk,' Sara cheerfully called out, and strapped both dogs into their leads, bringing the plastic bag for droppings.

This is so good, so many extra smells from this morning, Big Bro eagerly tugged to each spot.

There are some familiar smells here, but also a new one, Picasso pointed out.

Let me at it, I'll find out. As Big Bro pushed Picasso out of the way. *This is a big one, and hairy too. It eats a lot of dry food,* Big Bro deduced.

C'mon, it went this way. I can tell, it stepped in its own wee, let's follow. Picasso tried to track.

Nah, I think it went this way, Big Bro challenged Picasso.

'Let's go, you two. Plenty of things to smell today.' Sara urged them both on.

No, I want to go this way today. Picasso pulled on the harness, and when Sara did not yield, Picasso lowered her centre of gravity and stood her ground.

'Come on Picasso, let's go this way.' Sara tugged, but Picasso was equally strong and stubborn. They both stood their ground until, 'Okay, you win today, we'll go your way,' as Picasso bounced across the road.

Why do you argue with Mum? She always takes us on nice walks, Big Bro berated Picasso.

I wanted to go this way today. I can smell something over there – have a sniff, Big Bro, Picasso said.

Yeah, it's very faint, but it's there. I wonder what it is? Big Bro quizzed.

Let's find out, as Picasso led Big Bro and Sara on their walk.

The rest of the walk uncovered many different smells (dogs, cats, birds, rabbits, and leftover food people had thrown out). Picasso eventually led them home when she had enough.

We've met all sorts today, haven't we? There was Malcolm the Boxer – anyone could smell him and his slobbering jowls a mile away. And there was Teddy the Poodle – he is always so excited and keeps messing up everyone's track, Big Bro told Strife and Trouble.

And I smelt Murphy and Dusty – they always fight over who's going to mark the territory. It's no wonder they don't get very far, always competing with themselves, Picasso added.

And I think that big hairy one was a Labrador, plodded away like it did – I really think it was a Lab, Big Bro decided.

Are you two still playing the 'Pick the Smell' game? Aren't you tired of it yet? Strife was becoming bored with the usual monotonous game they played every time they went out for a walk.

Nah, this is fun, finding out about others. All of us are put on Earth for special things. We all take our own part: to lead, heal, follow, conquer, find a new path. It takes all sorts to make the world a better place; we all play our roles in our own special ways. Our strengths lie in our breeding. Our natural breeding gives us a good start, just like on that TV program. Natural selection helps to direct us into the best pathway for us. For instance, there are always groups: working dogs, hunting dogs, assistance dogs, toy dogs, lap dogs, guard dogs and plain lazy dogs. Big Bro was ready for another sermon. *Even when our natural abilities retire, others can take their place, like Rocket. He's a retired greyhound who is the biggest couch potato ever and has adapted into civilian life and would do anything for a smooch and cuddle.*

You mean that big one with elevated legs? His height scares me, but I know he's a big softie, Picasso reasoned.

Yes, there are other dogs that we must take care with, like Abbey or Sophie. Abbey is a Rhodesian Ridgeback – you can tell as her fur goes the other way on her back, almost like a mohawk. She's a rescue dog and was mistreated before she found her forever home. Sophie is a black Labrador and is in training for Guide Dogs. She lives with her foster family until she is old enough to do proper training, Big Bro continued.

What's a guide dog again? What do they do? Picasso asked.

Don't you remember the TV programs we have seen? A guide dog helps people with vision impairment. They are the eyes of the hoomans and they tell the hooman what to do, Strife piped up.

Oh yeah, I remember that program. They do other things too, don't they? Like telling if someone is at the door, or if the phone rings, or if an alarm goes off? They can do seeing and hearing as well, can't they? Picasso became more animated as she went on.

Yes, they can also tell if someone is going to be sick on the inside, like have a seizure or other chemical imbalance. There are other dogs that use their noses to search for lost humans, such as Bloodhounds or St. Bernards. Other dogs sniff out illegals, such as drugs or bombs or even illegal food at airports, Big Bro added.

Did someone say there are dogs that sniff out food? Can we get one? Trouble had finally found an interesting topic to discuss.

Big Bro carried on with his descriptions of the different breeds of dogs and their own special skills. *Dogs like Spot and Bubbles are inside cuddle dogs who love snuggling with their hoomans,* Big Bro beamed.

Let me see if I understand. Freddie is a Jack Russell who is very vocal and protective of his home and hooman. He often skips and hops when he goes walking. Chico's a Chihuahua that is also very protective of his family. He's a no-nonsense sort of dog, loves being the centre of attention, is very fierce and will take on almost anything. So, if I'm a Chihuahua Jack Russell cross, that makes me super protective, with the ability to take an important role in the family, and have the grace to bounce, hop and skip, but don't mess with me. I can pack a powerful punch, despite my size. I am direct and have specific desires. Am I close? Picasso clearly stated.

By George, I think you've got it! Yes, you are fast growing from puppy stage, and your skills have not been fully developed yet, but you are on the right track. Big Bro was pleased.

Yes, you are on your way, Picasso. Just remember that Trouble and I came to this family first, Strife reminded her.

I will, but I will excel over you in some areas. Be prepared for it, Picasso promised.

Picasso reflected on each breed's skills and saw herself rising above all others. She could be anyone she wants to be: a guard dog, a tracker dog, a sniffer dog, a guide dog, a lap dog, or anything else she could imagine. Picasso promised herself to test each area to the best of her abilities. She hoped to be an all-rounder one day. Some of these abilities were tested within the next week on the evening walk with Sara.

'Come on, Big Bro and Picasso, let's go down this way. We haven't been this way for a long time.' Sara steered the dogs towards the club on the corner.

No way. Not this way tonight, Mum. Can't you smell it? Picasso sniffed the air.

What? Oh yeah, I smell something too. It's not normal for this area, Big Bro agreed with Picasso.

We need to stop her, Big Bro. It's not good to go this way. I can smell danger, and fear, and anger, and panic in the air. It's a bad combination. It's coming from the club area. Quick, we must move Sara away from this area, or she'll get hurt. Picasso tugged on the lead.

Big Bro followed Picasso's lead and dragged Sara away from the club.

'Okay, okay, I got the picture, Picasso. You want to go this way. But sometimes it would be nice if we could go my way.' Sara followed the dogs away from the club and continued the evening walk.

The next day, when Sara and Tony were getting ready for work, the news on the radio started and they heard the announcer mention that the club was robbed last night at approximately eight forty-five. Three thieves with sawn off shotguns had tied the staff and some of the patrons up in the cool room while they stole money from the till and took the day's takings.

'Oh no. Did you hear that, Tony? The club was held up last night.' Sara was shocked.

'I hope nobody got hurt. Imagine something like this happening in our little community. They must have done this to get drugs. Everything ends in drugs these days.' Tony's moustache quivered as he raised his coffee cup to his lips.

'I know. You can always replace cash, and I'm sure they have insurance, but the stress and trauma the staff and patrons went through, it's just terrible. Why can't people live in peace and respect each other?' Sara questioned.

'It takes all kinds. I hope everyone will be okay,' Tony said and returned to the newspaper.

'Do you want to know a funny thing? I was taking the dogs for a walk last night, at the same time: eight forty-five. Picasso and Big Bro pulled me away from the club. I wanted to go past it, but the dogs were adamant. They dragged me away. Imagine if I didn't oblige. I would have seen the holdup and could have been shot at. How did they know? They saved me.' Sara and Tony looked at the dogs in amazement.

See, I told you they don't understand how smells work, Big Bro said.

Yeah, but did you also hear what Mum said? She said we saved her. I saved her. I'm living up to my breed's skills. I am good. Picasso basked in the pride of doing her job.

Chapter 19: Responsibilities

Picasso started taking her role within the family more seriously. Big Bro said every member played a part in the family and that we all need to pull together to make things happen. He had given her so much: his time, his wisdom, his experience. One day, Picasso hoped to repay some of the kindness. This happened sooner than expected.

Hey Big Bro, what's going on? You don't seem to be yourself lately. Picasso was concerned.

I'm okay Picasso. Just a little tired, and my mind often wanders off to past happy times. I guess I don't pay attention as much as I should, Big Bro confessed.

I think it's more often than not. You can rely on me to keep you and the family safe, Picasso offered.

Over the next few days, Picasso kept a close eye on her Big Bro. She slowly pieced together a few things: his hearing wasn't as good as it once was, his eyes didn't seem to work like they used to, his nose was losing its power. Out of respect for the knowledge he passed on to her, Picasso didn't want Big Bro to lose himself or his pride. Picasso identified some specific tasks she could do to alert Big Bro, and Sara and Tony too. It would be an honour to support him.

'A short walk for you two.' Sara clipped the leads on.

Both dogs were in front of Sara as they ambled along their favourite path, smelling the usual spots. Sara never noticed, but Picasso was ever attentive to her Big Bro.

Come this way, Big Bro. Just follow me and I'll pick out the really good spots to sniff, Picasso chatted.

Much obliged, Picasso. Sometimes all the smells blend into one and I have a hard time understanding what to follow, Big Bro confessed.

Don't worry, just follow me, I'll lead the way, Picasso offered.

And so it went every time they stepped out of the confines of the back yard and house. Picasso silently and discreetly led her Big Bro to the best smells to make sure he remained trouble free. Picasso did not stop on the outside walks, but also helped inside the house and yard. Picasso developed a specialised howl or bark to direct Big Bro into specific events.

It started the very next morning when the alarm clock trilled to wake Sara and Tony for work.

The allllarm. The allllarm. The allllarm, Picasso howled on cue.

This was loud enough to alert the whole household that the alarm clock had gone off. Big Bro roused himself from sleep, as did Trouble and Strife, to greet Sara and Tony getting out of bed.

'Well, that was something different. Did you change the sound on the alarm last night Sara?' Tony yawned.

'No, it's never done that before. Neither has Picasso. I wonder what was going through her head. Well, it certainly did the trick. We're up.' Sara wandered to the kitchen for feeding time. The cats were already waiting at their bowls.

Nice work, Picasso. Gave us plenty of time to get in line for breakfast. Trouble paced her area.

Yeah, thanks Picasso, you sounded just like the alarm. You got all the vowels extended perfectly, Strife chirped in.

Thanks, Picasso, for getting me up. I don't think they noticed me not hearing it. It created a brilliant diversion, Big Bro gushed.

Picasso had mastered the alarm clock and could alert the entire house when it went off. Picasso also managed other warnings as well. The 'Door' yap when someone knocked was easy to do. She had watched her Big Bro do it for over a year now.

One afternoon, Tony and Sara were out in the back yard putting new plants in the rockery when they heard Picasso howl. It sounded different to the morning howl as Sara listened to Picasso's sound more closely.

The phhhooooonnnee. The phhhooooonnnee. The phhhooooonnnee, Picasso called out over and over.

Sara stopped what she was doing and raced over to where Picasso was.

'Picasso, what's wrong? Are you hurt? Why were you howling? The alarm didn't go off, did it? What's happening?' Sara asked Picasso.

Picasso stood where she was for a moment, then led Sara into the house, right next to the phone and panted with a silly grin on her face. The phone had stopped ringing by now.

Mum won't get it just yet. She hasn't put two and two together yet. You need more time, Picasso, Strife said.

No, I'm sure she will get it. She knew it sounded different from the alarm – she just said so. I'll have to point out the phone to her more. Picasso stared from Sara to the phone.

It might take her some more time, keep doing what you're doing, Big Bro encouraged.

Sara shrugged and went back to the gardening. During their evening meal, Sara mentioned Picasso's howling that afternoon.

'I'm not sure what it meant. She wasn't hurt at all, just sitting there howling.'

'The alarm didn't go off accidentally? I told my work mates about her being the new alarm clock, and they didn't believe me,' Tony said.

'The alarm hadn't gone off. But this sound was different. It had a bit more 'oooo' sound to it.' Sara and Tony continued the discussion of animal noises throughout their meal and retreated to the kitchen to clean up the dirty plates.

What a waste, we could wash them cleaner than they could, Trouble complained.

Yes, and get all the leftover food, I suppose, Strife joined in.

Of course. The whole household is into recycling. Why waste good food? Trouble commented.

Once the dishes were done, Sara and Tony sat in their chairs to watch their favourite show. As the show was beginning, the phone rang, and Picasso started to howl.

The phhhoooonnee, The phhhoooonnnee. The phhhooooonnnee, Picasso called out.

'See? I told you. It's a different howl from the alarm clock.' Sara rose to answer the phone.

'Hello? Hi Trev, yes, he's here, just a minute ... Tony, it's Trevor,' Sara called out.

Sara handed the phone to Tony and heard some of the conversation with Trevor. Sara ignored the phone conversation, and turned her attention not to the TV, but to Picasso. Her howling stopped as soon as the phone stopped ringing.

'Are you telling me you were letting me know the phone was ringing?' Sara questioned Picasso.

She got it in one! Yippee, Big Bro and Strife shouted.

'What are you two barking and meowing at? I wasn't talking to you; I was talking to Picasso. So, Picasso, tell me about your howling? Is it my imagination or are you playing games with me?' Sara quizzed.

No, honest Mum, I'm not playing. I'm the new hearing eye dog. I saw it on TV that day. I'm an assistance dog now, honest. I've been a guard dog, a tracker dog and now an assistance dog, Picasso revealed.

Listen to her Mum. It's true. She does this to help me hear. But it also helps others too. Listen to Picasso, Big Bro pleaded.

'I'm not too sure about you. Sometimes, I think you are ganging up to conspire against me.' Sara returned her attention to the TV.

Don't give up, Picasso. She'll get there. She's just going through a change cycle. She doesn't want to believe it, but deep down inside she knows it to be true. She will understand and accept soon. It won't take her long, Big Bro uttered.

Don't stop, keep going, she's almost there, Picasso, Strife urged.

Why are you all chattering? I'm trying to nap, Trouble said.

I'll keep going, I promise not to give up. I'm determined to keep trying and be the best working dog, assistance dog, tracker dog, guard dog I can be, Picasso stated with pride.

Picasso took her responsibilities with such determination and care: alerting Big Bro of safety when going for walks, the alarm in the morning, the phone and visitors at the door. This helped hide Big Bro's failings in the seeing, hearing and smelling departments. Picasso would never let Big Bro's pride suffer. This was a huge task for a little dog to undertake, to be the carer and supporter for her Big Bro and the family. Such a responsibility prematurely aged Picasso, so that before she was two years, she was already sporting a greyish white face, and her strong black and tan colours were fading. Picasso reflected back on the 'Dogs with Jobs' TV show and tried to remember all the points they showed.

This show said it takes several years to train a dog to do a job. But I did it in a week. I should be featured on that show, Picasso complained.

We know what you are doing, and Big Bro appreciates it every day. You don't need much more praise than that. Keep going, and Mum and Dad will understand too. You're a good teacher, Picasso, Strife warmly stated.

I learnt from the best. I don't ever want my Big Bro to leave me. I can teach anyone these skills. Even Dusty and Murphy next door have caught on, Picasso said.

The next day, Sara was talking to her neighbour, Molly, over the fence when Molly's phone rang. They both heard Dusty and Murphy howling in the same tone Picasso used for her phone.

'Eich, I dunna know whee, but theere just started heowling when the pheone rings. I wunnder where they peaked it up frum?' Molly said in her strong Scottish accent as she went to get the phone.

'No idea, it seems almost too good to be true,' as Sara turned with a smirk and said to Picasso:

'It's true, you howl a certain way at the alarm in the morning, and a different way for the phone. You've even taught the neighbour's dogs to answer the phone the same way. Good on you. You are one smart cookie.' Sara smiled and headed for the house.

Big Bro, I've done it. I'm a teacher like you, Picasso gushed.

Picasso, you have excelled at teaching; you are now an educator. Go forth and educate others, Big Bro said with pride.

It took Sara and Tony several months to realise something was wrong with Big Bro. Picasso hid his secret well.

Chapter 20: Overcoming Setbacks — Resilience

'The builders will be here at seven thirty tomorrow morning, Sara. Make sure everything is safe as I don't want any broken things. Make sure the animals are also secured, I don't want them to get lost or run away,' Tony ordered Sara.

'Of course, I will. I'm just as concerned as you are. But I also believe and trust in the builders that they will do their very best,' Sara retaliated.

Very early the next day the builders set up shop in the back yard, with their power tools and work benches and odd assortment of items. They took no time at all to remove the old cladding from the exterior of the house.

What's going on, Big Bro? The noise is deafening, Picasso whimpered.

We're getting rid of the outside of the house. It looks too shabby, so we're getting nice new siding put up. But to me, the noise isn't that bad, Big Bro commented.

'Okay, dogs and cats, I'm off to work. You stay inside today as there is too much activity going on outside. You'll be safe in here.' Sara left the house and had a final chat to the workmen on her way out. They knew there were animals inside and would make sure no one escaped if they needed to get into the house.

During the day, a skip bin was delivered, and all the old cladding was removed and placed in the bin, ready for tomorrow's removal. By four thirty that afternoon, a truck delivering all the new cladding and insulation arrived and it was stored near the back shed. The builders checked and signed for the goods and packed up most of their tools. It was a long day.

That evening, Sara and Tony let the dogs and cats inspect the back yard and all the mess from the building area.

Can you smell what they had for lunch? Yummy sandwiches and some other things. I can smell fruit and some other things that aren't so nice, Trouble mentioned.

I can also smell some soft drinks, and water, and an orange, and of course them, Strife added.

They are really smelly too. They've sweat a lot over here where the workbench is, Picasso joined in.

Yes, it's a big job, but all the things they need are here. It seems well planned and organised. They need to do some fixing up before they put the new cladding on. See here, that's not right. Big Bro surveyed the work and pointed out areas that needed more work.

Oh, I see. It's all crooked and looks like it's been melted in one area. Strife viewed the area.

It's not melted, but it has deteriorated. Wood doesn't melt. There are bugs that eat wood – see here, there was a nest, but it's long gone now, Big Bro explained.

'Wow, they certainly worked hard today. It seems odd looking at a bare skeleton of the house. Now I understand why Martin warned me of any extras,' Sara commented as she also inspected the house with Tony and the animals.

'Martin always does excellent work, and this house has not had the best building buddies from way back,' Tony said as he started poking at odd bits.

'Would you please stop what you're doing and let the experts do their thing. Every time you try to help, you make a bigger mess. I can't afford for you to make a bigger mess,' Sara snapped.

'You never had much faith in me, did you?' Tony challenged.

'I'm only stating facts. You are not a builder, so don't try to think you are and start doing things,' Sara answered back.

'Just wanting to help them out,' Tony admitted.

'You'd help them out if you would just leave it alone. They have their plan of building, leave them to it.' Sara was exasperated.

The building continued for several days and the fixing up of odd bits had finished. The workmen also tidied up behind them so that they had more room to move after each task was over. Now, it was time to start the cladding. Sara always left the house open so they could use the facilities. Tea, coffee and biscuits were left out for them on the kitchen counter for their break.

Sometimes, the animals ventured outside and inspected every move the builders made. They were fascinated by the activities and the movements they were doing. One particularly fine afternoon, Big Bro, Picasso, Trouble and Strife were having a snooze outside. The cats had found a safe place away from the noise. Big Bro had found a space on the lawn not far from the back door and was having a wonderful nap.

'Got to go back into town and grab a few more screws to finish off the side. Won't be long, be back soon,' Martin called to Rick as he swung himself into the ute and started reversing out the yard.

In a split second, Picasso woke up and saw her Big Bro in the way of the ute and started to bark to wake him up.

Get up Big Bro, get up. You're in the way. Stop ute. You're going to run over my Big Bro ... stoooppppp! Picasso shrieked.

Thump, bang. The ute bumped over something. Martin stopped the ute and got out.

'Oh, no, I've run over the dog. Rick, help me get the dog out.' Rick rushed over and both men dragged the dog from under the ute. A sigh of relief was shown as the dog was still alive. 'Quick, help me put the dog in the front seat. I've got to take him to the vet to get checked out.' Both men place Big Bro in the front seat.

No, leave my Big Bro with me. Where are you taking him to? Why did you run over him? Picasso screamed as she saw her Big Bro go away in the ute.

Rick tried to calm Picasso down and eventually caught her and put her inside the house to be safe. Both cats followed.

Martin drove to the nearest vet, parked and cradled Big Bro in his arms as he ran through the door.

'Help, I've just run over the dog with my one-tonne ute. He's still alive, but I need you to check him out. Please let him be okay,' Martin called out.

The vet ushered Martin and Big Bro through to an examination room. After several minutes, the vet assured Martin that the dog was fine.

'Such a strong dog this one. He's sore and will have some bruising, but it doesn't seem like anything has been broken or torn. Have him take these pain killers to ease the bruising and soreness. Let him take it easy for the next few days. For an old dog such as him, I was expecting worse – but he's a very tough dog. Kelpies always are,' the vet instructed.

The vet gave Martin the tablets; Martin paid for the consult and took Big Bro back home. He settled him inside before going to see Sara at her work. Sara came rushing home to see Big Bro.

'Big Bro, what's happened to you? You poor brave soul. You need to rest and take it easy,' Sara crooned over him.

I'm sorry, Big Bro, I'm sorry. I wasn't paying attention enough. I didn't see the ute back up until it was too late. I'm sorry you got hurt, Picasso cried.

I know it's not your fault, Picasso, it was an accident. These things happen sometimes. It's nobody's fault, and I got care. Don't hold a grudge; forgive. I am very sore and need to rest now, Big Bro whispered.

I will never leave your side, ever again, Picasso promised and vowed to watch over him as he often watched over her.

Chapter 21: Alternative Avenues

The entire household cared over big Bro throughout the next few weeks. Luckily, the building had finished, and Big Bro could safely go into the back yard. Not many old dogs can handle being run over by a ute. Whether Big Bro was feeling his age of sixteen, or because of the accident, his walks became shorter and shorter. Even getting his back legs working in unison was a challenge.

I'm very sore and it hurts, Picasso. Somehow, we need to let Mum and Dad know I hurt, Big Bro admitted to Picasso.

I'll look after you, always. Next time we go for a walk, I want you to whimper and shuffle your feet. Look down at the ground and concentrate. That might give the desired effect to get help, Picasso instructed Big Bro.

That evening, Sara took both dogs out for a walk. They didn't get very far when Big Bro started to shuffle and omitted a whimper and even included a stumble.

That's it, Big Bro, nice touch adding the stumble, whispered Picasso.

It wasn't meant to be, it just happened. I think I jarred my back leg and tail area. It stings, Big Bro gasped.

'Big Bro, I think you're not doing too well. This is not right. I've never known you to whimper. You must be in so much pain. Can you make it back to the house?' Sara asked.

Sara patted Big Bro's head and back. When she got to his back legs, Big Bro let out another whimper. Sara hoped she wouldn't have to carry Big Bro back – he weighed twenty-five kilos and would be a struggle.

You did good, Big Bro, you whimpered at just the right time, Picasso escorted Big Bro home.

It wasn't luck, I really really hurt. I felt it. I'm so sore, Picasso. I don't know how much more I can handle. I don't want to make a fuss. Big Bro concentrated on getting back to the house.

'Big Bro is in a bad way. He's in so much pain. I'm taking tomorrow off to go back to his vet. Maybe there is something they can do for him.' Sara was worried for her long-term companion.

'If he's in that bad a way, maybe we could put him out of his misery?' Tony suggested.

'No way, it's almost Christmas and you know how much he loves his Christmas. I want him to have one final one. Peter, the vet, will be able to do something to make him be okay until just after Christmas. Peter likes Big Bro, he'll understand,' Sara challenged.

The next day, Sara drove to where Big Bro's vet was and waited to see Peter. Sara explained what had happened and how important it was for Big Bro to see in one last Christmas.

'It's only two weeks away, surely something can be done for him?' Sara pleaded.

'Have you heard of alternative medicine? We know about it from a human standpoint, but it has also been used on animals. Do you want to try?' Peter asked.

'Sure, I'll try anything to help him,' Sara admitted.

'Bring him here. This is called acupuncture and it will settle any nerve and muscle issues in his hind legs. He needs to rest for at least five minutes. Try not to let him move. I'll be back in a little while,' Peter said.

Peter placed Big Bro on a mat on the ground and inserted several needles into Big Bro. He left the room, closing the door behind him. Big

Bro tried to look at what was twitching him Sara soothingly discussed all the happy moments in his life.

Peter returned, removed the needles and flipped Big Bro onto his other side. He inserted new needles in similar places from the other side. Sara could see the needles twitching and crooned to Big Bro again. A short time later, Peter returned and removed the needles.

'If you want, he can have another treatment in two days' time. In the meantime, here are some natural remedies. Let him have two little black balls three times a day. Be warned that these are very powerful, and he must not get too exerted from this. If he starts to jump and play around, you must calm him down and reduce the dose. He must not overexert himself, is that clear? The instructions are on the sheet,' Peter directed.

'Thank you so much, Peter, I think he feels better and more alert now. I'll book in for another acupuncture session.'

Sara booked Big Bro in and drove back home. She showed Big Bro the little beads, and semi hid them in his evening meal. They were scoffed down in no time. Big Bro rested.

What did they do to you, Big Bro? What happened? Picasso asked that night.

I'm not sure what it was, but they laid me on my side and put little things on me. I felt such a rush of warmth and release between these things. I felt like the soreness and pain was leaving me. Then they did the same to my other side. I've never felt this kind of treatment, but it seemed to work, Big Bro explained.

So, you feel better? They didn't give you a needle or shove something awful down your throat or up your bum? Strife asked.

No, it wasn't like a normal visit, but I think they used something like a needle, but it wasn't. I'm not sure, but it felt great. I'm tired now, I'll see you in the morning, Big Bro sighed.

Over the next few days, Big Bro's life went on a definite upswing. He attended a few more acupuncture sessions and the little black beads were doing so well that he was jumping around like a young pup. Sara tried to calm him down, but Big Bro thought otherwise.

I feel so great. No pain. Full of energy. I feel like I could do anything, Big Bro sang.

Hey, Big Bro, I think you should calm down, like Mum said. I don't want to see you get overworked, Strife cautioned.

Nah, I feel great, no pain, Big Bro sang.

I think she's right. Come here and sit down and tell me stories from long ago, Picasso tempted Big Bro.

Eventually Big Bro did and started telling stories from long ago. Sara also started reducing the little black beads.

The Christmas tree and decorations went up and Big Bro continued with his stories. He also noticed that Sara was slowly stopping his little black beads and the pain was creeping back in. Still, he was excited to see another Christmas – his favourite time of the year. This year was special; he received three squeak toys, some chews and tennis balls.

Slowly, in the New Year, Big Bro deflated and felt every moment of his sixteen-and-a-half years. He started to lose control of his back legs and would often fall over.

Give him the black beads, give him back the drugs, Picasso yelled at Sara.

'Oops, Big Bro, go slow so your back legs can catch up with your front ones,' Sara helped Big Bro to his feet again.

Thank you for caring for me Sara, I don't mean to be a nuisance, Big Bro apologised.

Don't apologise to her, she stopped your happy drugs, Picasso gave Sara the evil eye.

No, do not hold grudges, as they eat you up from the inside. Mum has done everything possible to make my last few weeks more enjoyable. I shall miss her, as I shall you, and Strife, and Trouble, and all the other friends we have met in our lives, Big Bro philosophised.

What do you mean? Are you telling me that this is the end? No, it can't be. If Sara just gives you some more black beads, it will be alright. Picasso became worried.

I'm tired. Let me rest with my memories, Picasso. Big Bro lay down and rested.

Over the next few days, Big Bro became worse and had to drag himself up all the time. He even made a few accidents and was mortified. Picasso saw the mistakes and tried to cover them up by dragging her blanket over the mess so no one would see.

'I think it's time to call Peter over. There is no more quality of life. I sense he feels very embarrassed that his private bits aren't working, and he can barely stand now,' Sara admitted to Tony that night.

'Do you think he's really that bad, Sara?' Tony did not want to hear the truth.

'Look at him. I've never seen a sadder and pain-riddled dog in all my life. It's kinder to let him go. I've got tomorrow off from work, I'll take him to all his favourite spots in the morning, and I'll ask Peter to do a house call in the afternoon. Can you please dig a hole in the back yard – in his preferred spot,' Sara calmly asked Tony.

The next morning, Sara grabbed her car keys and called out to Big Bro and Picasso.

'Come on, Big Bro, and you too, Picasso. We're going on a drive,' Sara stated.

Sara lifted Big Bro into the back seat. She drove to the forest area where Big Bro spent much of his younger years visiting, and then to the creek, where he often swam on a hot summer's day. They then visited an open paddock with cows in the far corner. All the places he enjoyed and loved. Sara carried Big Bro everywhere so he could have one last visit.

Thank you, Sara, for giving me a wonderful life with you and the rest of my family. I appreciate everything you have done for me, Big Bro stated with love in his face, despite the pain he felt.

It's not over yet, Big Bro. Hang on, Picasso whimpered.

No, Picasso, it's time to go. I've taught you everything I know. Use the knowledge well. I shall miss you. Look after the others for me when I'm gone, Big Bro gasped.

That afternoon, Peter visited and confessed, 'He's not ready to go yet, but I decided to come anyway. Where's the special boy?'

Peter looked at Big Bro and was startled to see the degree of deterioration in the back half of his body.

'Sorry, I didn't know he was this bad. I'll just get the stuff from my van,' Peter went back to his van, and retrieved his medical bag.

'We have a space for him up the back,' Tony uttered through gasps.

Peter nodded and picked Big Bro up by himself and carried him towards the back garden. This is no mean feat considering he felt like a dead weight. Peter gently placed Big Bro down beside the awaiting hole.

What's he doing here? What's going on? Picasso asked Strife and Trouble. Strife ran away; Trouble just stared, then retreated to the house.

'This is it. I'll put the tourniquet around his arm and then will inject him with the serum. I'm warning you; he will go every fast. Be prepared,' Peter explained as he put the tourniquet on his arm and punctured it with a needle.

No, don't do this, let him go. Get up and run Big Bro, Picasso cried.

Sara and Tony watched Peter working with Big Bro. Sara bent down to gently pat Big Bro's head and face.

'I shall miss you, Big Bro – there has never, nor will there ever be, another dog quite like you Be at peace and pain free,' Sara blubbered.

No, no, no, no, this is not going to happen. Stay away from my Big Bro, V-E-T, Picasso wailed.

Peter reached into his bag and took out a vial of thick green liquid, inserted the needle and drew the required amount.

Noooo, this is no good. Run away, Big Bro, run away. Don't let them do this – I'm sorry I didn't do my job well enough – I'm sorry that I let you get run over – give me another chance and you won't regret it. Don't do this, I'm sorry, so sorry, don't kill him, I smell death in that needle. Stop ... don't do it to him, help me, anyone, help me, Picasso wailed.

Life lessons rushed past Picasso's mind: all the things her Big Bro had taught her, all the learning, fun, laughter, peace, food and play. *Nooo, not the needle – it has death all over it, get up and runaway, Big Bro,* Picasso panicked and instinctively knew she had a matter of moments left. *I want to tell you how grateful I am, and how much I appreciate you for all your life lessons, company and companionship over the past four years. I will never forget you. You mean that much to me. Big Bro? Big Bro, can you hear me?* Picasso screamed.

The needle was inserted into his left arm. Big Bro felt a little sting, and then relaxed. He could smell and feel Sara near his head, he could hear Picasso calling out to him, he knew Tony was there, and Peter was by his side – the one who gave him the little black beads to make the pain go away. Focus faded and all the tension in his body released. He felt no pain, just a sensation that he was no longer attached to the earth. He sensed himself floating off into the fluffy clouds. Sounds of Earth were a distant memory. He was off to his next journey in the sky, as his body was left behind.

I'm so sorry, Big Bro, help me to save you, run away, there's still time! Picasso called out.

Picasso noticed that Big Bro's body had drooped and relaxed from the lack of strain in his body and face. A faint shadow of a smile lingered on Big Bro's mouth. Peter removed the needle and held a cotton bud on the crook of Big Bro's arm. With his free hand, he reached for the stethoscope and put one end into his ears, and one end on Big Bro's heart. He listened for a few minutes and murmured.

'He's gone,' Peter quietly stated.

Peter repacked his bag whilst gasping breaths were heard from Sara and Tony as huge droplets of tears streamed from their eyes. Peter gently picked Big Bro up and placed him in the hole.

Noooo, that is for plants and flowers – not Big Bro, how can you do this? How can you let him do this, Mum and Dad? You are bad people. Stop, what have you done to my Big Bro? Picasso was frantic.

Peter picked up the shovel leaning against the fence and placed the first shovel of dirt on top of Big Bro.

Noooo, don't bury him, he'll come back to me. Nooo, stop. Big Bro, I'm sorry, Picasso pleaded.

Peter continued to shovel the dirt onto Big Bro.

Oh, my Big Bro … I'm sorry, I'm so sorry. Ooohhhhh, Picasso cried.

Picasso continued to cry inconsolably for the loss of her Big Bro and the realisation that he would no longer be with her in her life. Tony grabbed the shovel from Peter, shook his hand, and commenced to shovel the rest of the dirt over Big Bro. Sara had not moved and was still kneeling, tears gushing down her face.

'I'm sorry. He was one of the best dogs I've ever seen. I'll see myself out.' Peter grabbed his bag and walked towards his van, his head hanging low.

Serves you right – you killed my Big Bro. I will always hate you, Picasso wailed after Peter, and glanced back at the burial site.

Chapter 22: Challenges Ahead

A heavy black cloud hung over the household for several days. Very little talking was heard. Each member of the household was dealing and coping with the recent event in their own way. The hole had been dug and filled. Sara had planted a purple diosma over the site, one of Big Bro's favourite plants. Motions of life were performed, but without heart. Luckily, the food for the animals kept coming. It was discerning to see only three bowls of food instead of the usual four. No matter what was attempted, the loss of Big Bro touched all members of the family.

'I'll go and pay the vet bill on the way to work today,' Sara said flatly.

Why would you want to pay for the death of my Big Bro? It's the V-E-T who should pay – how could anyone do such a thing? Picasso complained through her tears.

It's what some V-E-T-S do, Picasso. Sometimes, they have to do these really hard things. Big Bro was brave, and he never complained. But even you could see he was in a bad way, Strife comforted.

Why did they stop with the mini needles, and the little black beads? They were helping him, Picasso argued.

They were only prolonging his life. Giving him some more pain free time. But he had come to the end. You saw it on his face and on his body – he was just holding himself together. They really did the humane thing, Strife soothed.

Don't tell me about being humane – they're inhumane – they killed my Big Bro – I will never have him with me again, ever. I thought they loved him, and me. How could they do this? Picasso wailed herself to sleep.

Picasso's sleep was shattered and tormented by reliving all the moments she had had with her Big Bro., and nightmares of being punished for not looking after him and allowing the ute to run over him. This was her cross to bear; it was all her fault. Her soulmate had gone, and now she had no more purpose in life. The invisible blanket smothered her sadness; her whole epicentre of existence had been wiped from her life.

'Poor Picasso is really doing it tough, isn't she?' Sara commented.

'Give her time, that's all she needs, Sara. Just more time,' Tony consoled.

'They say time heals everything, but there is still a gaping hole where someone, or some dog, has touched your life. I don't think you could ever forget them. I suppose their memories live on forever. I miss him though,' Sara admitted.

'I know; I miss him too. We have a lot of great memories to keep him alive in our hearts,' Tony reasoned.

'I want to cuddle and kiss Picasso, but she runs off. She won't even go out the back door,' Sara stated.

'Just give her time and let her come to you,' Tony assured Sara.

Why would I want to cuddle and get a kiss from you? You took away my Big Bro. I want no part of this. What if you suddenly decide to throw me in the hole and bury me too, like you did with Big Bro? I'm not doing this – stay away from me. I don't trust you, Picasso grumbled and complained.

They are remorseful – can't you tell? They're trying to ease the loss. Let them, Strife explained.

What? And side with the killers. No way, I will keep this up as long as I can, Picasso promised.

I suggest you don't, as it will fester inside you and eat you up. You'll be making yourself sick. Remember what Big Bro said? Don't let things fester-move on and forgive, Strife warned.

Yeah, don't let it get to you. Save the room for food. I miss him too, but it was his time to go. We all have our time. We just need to make the most of what we have every day, Trouble chimed in, and then visited her food bowl.

I still hate them for doing what they did. I will make sure they never forget. They can't get close to me, so I will continue to hide under the bed where they can't get at me. I have nightmares every night and miss him so much it hurts. The back yard has death all over it. I'm scared that they might put me in the ground too. Picasso retreated to under the bed and cried herself to sleep.

'I'm still worried about Picasso; she's still not eating, she won't go into the back yard, and she doesn't go for a walk like she used to. How do you help a little dog who's grieving like she is?' Sara asked Tony.

'I don't know Sara, if she doesn't come good in a few days, we might have to take her to Peter – maybe he could give her something?' Tony confirmed.

Strife immediately visited Picasso under the bed, *Hey Picasso, Sara and Tony are really worried about you. If you don't pick up, they'll take you to Peter. You know, the V-E-T. I know it's hard, but you have to make an effort.* Strife was concerned.

No, they want to get rid of me too. I never want to see another V-E-T again. I don't trust them – perhaps they have poisoned my food and want to kill me too? Picasso dared.

Well, then, you have to start socialising again, Strife commented.

Why can't people leave me alone in peace? Picasso wailed.

We're all worried about you. How about you try to make little steps and have something to eat and go out for a short walk, then you can have your peace under the bed with your memories? Strife tried to instil some of Big Bro's philosophical ideals with Picasso.

Well, I am hungry a bit, and it might do me good to go out – but only in little doses, okay? Picasso made an agreement.

Sure, I guess I'll stick with cat food again. I was beginning to like dog food, Trouble piped up.

Night-time was the time when Picasso ventured out from underneath the bed. She sniffed every inch of the house, for a smell of Him, and absorbed this to keep her memories alive. She reflected on her life with him over and over. Keeping these memories alive comforted Picasso, but it also disrupted her, especially those memories of the final few months. The past four years of her life were so filled with Big Bro: her educator, mentor, confidant, friend, brother, soulmate. Picasso took several more weeks processing his life lessons and his company. She reviewed many of his monologues in her mind.

We have gone through so many things. I hope I don't forget his teachings. He's been such a big part of my life. How I miss him, how I failed him, how I didn't do well enough for him. So much of me has died without him. How can I go on without him? He would never want me to cry so much. He would want me to keep going, so I will for him – and him alone. I owe this to him. I don't know what to do next – he always made suggestions. Now, I will have to make my own decisions and plan my day. This is so new to me, Picasso reasoned.

Slowly, Picasso returned to some form of her usual life, but still refused to go into the back yard.

I can see you're trying. Good for you. But why don't you come into the back yard? It's so peaceful here, Strife praised the little dog.

I cannot go there – that is the scene of such destruction, betrayal and death. How could anyone ever think I would want to go there? Picasso was horrified.

I'm sure it's not that bad. I want to show you something – something that might make you happy, Strife chirped.

No, not me – not yet. I'm not ready for death. Picasso turned towards her basket, snuggled up and went to sleep.

Big Bro's aura and personal scent in the house had been wafting out, so that there was only a faint trace of him now. It wasn't until the beginning of autumn that Picasso decided to venture into the back yard.

It was a pleasant Saturday afternoon and Sara was reading a book in the patio area. Sara often left the door to the house open so the dogs and cats could enter and leave at their own pace. Picasso stood at the doorway, sniffed the air and could not detect any poisons or death smells.

I must be strong. Big Bro would not appreciate me holding a grudge like this. I have been very sick for several months, but now I need to become well. Big Bro loved life and the smell of the flowers, trees, ground, people, greeting all his friends, stopping and saying hello to everyone, and enjoying every moment. He would not like to see me being so sad all the time. I will make this effort – I owe it to him, Picasso encouraged herself as she moved a few paces outside.

Looking around, she saw the back yard with a new set of eyes. So much had grown over the last few months, she almost didn't recognise it.

Glad to see you venturing out, Picasso. Come, nobody will hurt you. Come and get reacquainted with the back yard. We've had a whole heap of changes. The magpie family's young have grown, the willy wagtails have been visiting as well as the wild rabbits from the field across the way. Come and see, Strife eagerly whispered so Sara would not be disturbed.

It took several more minutes for Picasso to take a few steps to the edge of the paving. Looking around the yard, her eyes found the offending death scene. But what she saw was not a heap of dirt, shovels and her dead mentor, but a beautiful garden of flowers and shrubs. This confused her as she was expecting something else.

See, I told you weeks ago to come out and have a look. It's wonderful, isn't it? Strife proudly stated.

I can't believe it's the same place. What happened? Picasso was awestruck.

I told you. Tony and Sara planted some plants – all the things Big Bro loved. It's a memorial shrine to him. Go and have a look, Strife urged.

No, not yet. Let me just look for now. I can't smell him or the V-E-T. Picasso sniffed the air.

Nah, only good smells now, Trouble said.

'Oh, are you finally coming out for a visit, Picasso? Why don't you come and look at Big Bro's diosma bush? It was his favourite. And we've planted some plumbago and geraniums too. He loved them all. Come with me.' Sara put her book down and strolled to his back garden.

Picasso crouched down and started backing up. Both Strife and Trouble followed Sara to the far corner and the garden.

Come on, nothing to be worried about, Picasso, Trouble and Strife called back.

Picasso took a deep breath and tenderly took a few steps at a time towards the back garden.

I must embrace all the good things about my Big Bro. I must understand the wisdom of the world according to my Big Bro. I must remember all the things he taught me. I must learn to forgive. Picasso used these mantras.

Picasso soon realised she was half-way there. She hesitated and looked back towards the house. Her escape route was clear – if she needed it. Picasso took another deep breath and slowly crept forward to where Sara, Strife and Trouble were sitting at the back garden. If Picasso could sneak up, then they would not have time to catch her. Picasso went as close as she dared and peered into the garden filled with beautiful flowers and plants.

Glad you could make it, Picasso. This is a peaceful place that belongs to our Big Bro, Strife stated.

It is beautiful – he would have been very pleased, Trouble added.

It was his way – he was in so much pain in the end. He wouldn't have wanted to go on any longer. You must see that, Strife rationalised.

I did know for a long time, I suppose, but didn't want to admit it. I knew his body parts no longer worked, and he was embarrassed by his accidents. I also suppose Sara and Tony and even Peter did everything they could to help him. I must be grateful for that, Picasso admitted.

And you told me Sara took you and Big Bro to all his favourite places that morning. That's gotta count for something too, Trouble chimed.

And he had his last Christmas with us. He loved Christmas, didn't he? I guess his last few weeks were filled with dignity, grace and respect. I will always miss him. Picasso looked towards Sara.

'Oh, hello Picasso. I'm glad you've come to this special place. It was Big Bro's favourite spot to have a snooze and watch the world go by. I hope you approve. We've planted all his favourite flowers. He should be happy here. No more pain or suffering. He is at peace now.' Sara reached for the diosma and fingered the flowers.

Picasso continued to look at Sara, and then the garden. She sat for a few moments before going back to the house. It would take her several more visits to be fully comfortable with the place where her Big Bro left his mark.

Chapter 23: I will, for Chicken

The bonds that Picasso, Strife and Trouble shared rested peacefully in the back yard. All three animals now lived together in harmony. Nobody could ever replace Big Bro; many of his teachings, beliefs, values and ethics were at the very core of their lives. Trust, belief and respect in each other grew immensely within the family.

Part of working together is finding everyone's strengths and weaknesses, and using their abilities to their very best, and includes tolerance and acceptance. Big Bro empowered all individuals to follow these basic rules. The three animals spent many a night chattering about the differences in the world.

It seems everyone has a different way to do things. We can't all be perfect in the same thing. It would be too boring, Strife began.

I think it also is because of our unique body size. Trouble admired her girth.

Or it could be our upbringing, Picasso added.

Or it could be a whole bunch of things. I don't think it is any one particular thing, but lots of things put together. Trouble amazed everyone with this piece of knowledge.

I've been listening to and reading Mum's study books. She's doing something on personality right now. I think personality tells us who is going to lead, who is going to follow, who is not going to listen, or go off on a different pathway. That's okay, as everyone needs to do what they are good at, Strife added with air.

Maybe each of us has a special inner glow that makes us do this personality thing a special way? Picasso thought. Perhaps her diamonde microchip on the inside helped with this?

I wonder how many personalities there are? Trouble tried to count on her paw.

Sometimes, I think is this my true personality, or am I supposed to be someone else? I wonder how we really know? How do we really find out who we are supposed to be? Picasso wondered.

Finding out who you are relies on different things. The trick is finding out what that special thing is to you, and to then try to make a difference in the world, Strife continued.

But what if you want to be more like someone else? What if you want to try to live up to someone else's standards? Like Big Bro? Could you do that then? Picasso blurted.

I don't think so. Flattery and memory are nice, but I think you also have to be true to yourself and be yourself. Strife gazed at her sister.

You need to be you. Nobody has experienced exactly what you've gone through. They might understand, but they truly don't know the full picture. Trouble started grooming her rotund figure.

That's right. Trouble and I are twins, but I don't know a hundred percent exactly what's going through her mind. I mean, I can guess, but she's still her own person, Strife commented.

So, we each have to figure out what makes us us, and then do the best we can. Yes, I can imagine Big Bro exploring this. Picasso settled down to think about her Big Bro.

'What are you studying now, Sara? There's a lot of books and charts. It doesn't make sense to me,' Tony said.

'Oh no, it's wonderful. We're still doing personality, but also looking at motivation within each personality type. It's very exciting. I mean, figuring out what makes people tick, what makes them want or don't want to do things. What gives them the extra bit to go further, it's fascinating,' Sara said breathlessly.

'Well, I think it's a whole bunch of malarkey. People are people. Take them as they are. I'm going to the shed,' Tony left in a huff.

'It's not malarkey, there's a science to this and it does work. It helps to figure out what people are predisposed to do. It's helped in a variety of circles. It's a fascinating subject and will assist with my new career choice. The drama with Cheryl and Mick at work helped to catapult me into this area,' Sara called out to Tony as he retreated to his shed.

Sara continued to study, scribbling notes down or highlighting passages in her books. Several hours were spent pouring over these books almost every night.

See, I told you it works in a wide range of things. Strife pointed to Sara.

What do all those words say? Can you read? Picasso wondered.

No, I can't read their language, but I can read her body language, and she's a fast learner. Have you seen her discuss how people hold their body on the TV? And how she predicts their movements? She's getting good at it now, Strife puffed.

So, what motivates your personality? Picasso asked.

Well, I'm the smart one, if you haven't already figured it out. I use my brains to think things through and figure out how to do things. I watch and learn from others: their routine, their ways, stuff like that. Trouble, on the other hand, uses her bulk and brawn in every situation, Strife said.

So, what is my personality? What is my motivation? I feel as if I've changed so much that I'm not fully sure, Picasso admitted.

Well, you were an extremely annoying little dog at one point in time. I despised you, and no matter what Big Bro said, I still hated you and wanted you gone. But now, you have changed – for the better. You took good care of Big Bro when he lost his sight and hearing. You looked out for him. You started earning your brownie points from then. You've started to show your real personality, Strife reflected.

So, am I a helping dog, or a tracker dog, or a guard dog, or a dog that has a job like on TV? If Big Bro is gone, who am I going to help next? Picasso wondered.

Who else is here to help? Trouble sat on Sara's papers on the floor and started washing herself.

Mum? Is that my next job? Looking after Mum? But she doesn't really need me, does she? Picasso reviewed all the things Sara had done.

Maybe your next job is to keep her company? Ever thought of that? Strife joined her sister in grooming.

Wow, keeping company? That's a new one. Picasso laid down to watch Sara scribble on papers, read and sometimes colour.

It's not really new, it's called companion dogs, Strife muttered between her licking.

Picasso fell asleep thinking about personality and where she fitted in. Her Big Bro taught her some great things, and now she was starting to fully understand his lessons: be useful, make every day count, enjoy what you do, be kind and respectful, tolerant and accepting of others and their ways, see things from other perspectives, take time out to have some fun. She reflected on the various personalities out there and what makes people 'tick.' Picasso made connections between personalities and breeds of dogs, but what about humans? Are their personalities harder to identify?

Sara completed her study for the night and tried to put her books away but could not rescue her papers on the floor as two tabby cats posed as excellent paper weight and would not budge. She left them where they were, but quietly tidied her study materials around the barriers, and preceded to go to the kitchen to prepare the evening meal. Sara put the chicken in the oven to cook, prepared the vegetables and tidied the kitchen.

An hour later, the animal's inbuilt alarm clock sounded, and they roused from their nap, stretching and yawning to get the last of their dreams out of the way. A most pleasant smell drifted through the house, and Strife, Trouble and Picasso followed the beautiful aroma.

OOOh chicken for dinner tonight. How wonderful. Trouble sat in the best spot in the middle of the kitchen.

No, it's mine, I llloooooovvveee chicken. Picasso salivated.

There's enough for all of us. I hope she doesn't give us the regular food. Let's hold out for chicken, Strife planned.

I love chicken – it's my favourite. I'll do anything for chicken, Picasso stated as she took her spot on the kitchen floor.

So, does loving chicken also show us personality? Trouble asked.

I think it has more to do with motivation, Strife commented.

What's that? Picasso asked.

I think motivation also goes with personality, but it's a little different. It is a special thing that each one of us wants so much it hurts, and we will do anything for it, Strife lectured.

Can you have a few things? 'Cause I love food and sleeping, Trouble offered.

Yes, Trouble, I think we have your personality and motivation understood, giggled Strife.

Picasso waited patiently for the chicken to be cooked and thought of her special motivation. That's easy, Picasso thought, chicken. Chicken was the best motivator in the world. There are other foods that Picasso loved, but nothing came close to chicken. You could eat it raw, grilled, fried, in a stir fry, boiled, steamed, sliced, diced, cubed, minced, bone in, bone out, cold, hot, crispy, soft, dry, wet, shaved, chunky, fresh, stale or any other way. It was wonderful; it put everyone in a state of euphoria. Picasso could breathe it into her very soul; it crept underneath her skin, into her pores and muscles, tissues, tendons and coursed through her veins. Her body and mind hummed with the very mention of chicken. She would do almost anything for chicken.

'I don't know what it is, but every time we have chicken, they come out of the woodwork,' Tony said to Sara as he came in from working in the shed.

'Just like you? The internal body clock must be working. Just another ten minutes or so and it will be ready,' Sara smiled.

'They're easy to work with and predict. Just mention 'chicken' and they'll be here,' Tony twitched his moustache.

'This follows what I'm studying at university: people's personalities and what makes them tick. Next week, we'll be looking at motivation techniques. It's fascinating,' Sara pulled the plates and cutlery out of the drawers.

'Well, I still think it's rubbish, going to university, you'll end up with a big debt. Mightn't even get a job out of it. Why can't you be happy with what you had?' Tony whinged.

'I'm tired of having limited minimum wages jobs – I want to better myself and to learn more. We never seem to have any spare money to do anything, like take a holiday or fix the car. I had a chat with the lady from the Cheryl and Mick case, and she steered me into becoming a HR workplace negotiator. I want to prepare for my future and have financial stability. I can't do it with the job I have now. I will get there, with or without your help. The day you stop learning is the day you start dying,' Sara affirmed the last line.

'Just don't go reaching too far. You might fall,' Tony warned.

'I won't fall – I have only one way to go, up. This will help me get to where I want to go. It will help with my new career choice. Nobody's going to stop me achieving,' Sara said determinedly.

See, I said you could help Mum. This is her motivation. It blends in with her personality. You can help her achieve what she wants, Strife added.

You mean, help her study? But I can't read her books, Picasso stuttered.

No, all you have to do is 'be there.' Sara will appreciate your support, Strife reasoned.

Is the chicken ready yet? I'm hungry. All this talk and not enough action, Trouble complained.

Chapter 24: Unhappiness

Over the next few months, a blanket of tension covered the house. Sara's study books and papers had grown into a huge pile, and the dining room table had been taken over with it. Sara juggled work, household tasks, study and exam revision. Tony complained about the state of the house and Sara's study habits. He would love things to go back to how they were. The animals felt it but carried on in their own way. Trouble continued to sleep and eat, Strife watched for cues in personality, whereas Picasso was just there for Sara. She felt the building tension but was torn between Sara and Tony. She tried her best.

Why is this happening? Neither Mum nor Dad are happy anymore. They are always snapping at each other. It's not nice. I have no place to escape this, Picasso complained to Strife.

I know; I feel like I need to walk on eggshells. I can see both sides of the argument, but both sides are not listening to each other as well. They're both changing and growing – Mum more than Dad. I don't know how to fix this, Strife confessed.

'C'mon Picasso, time for a walk.' Sara collected the lead, harness and dog dropping bag, and hooked Picasso up. On their walk, they spent a few minutes in silence before Sara started mumbling to herself. Picasso listened.

'Oh, this is not how I thought my life would go. I want to be better and go places, but I feel trapped here. My job is okay, but it just pays the bills. I need more to live on and do things with. I have another four subjects left at university, so hopefully I can start looking for a better paying job.' Sara looked down at Picasso. 'I guess you can't understand any of this. You just wag your tail and pant. Must be nice to be a dog, you have no pressures in life.' Sara sighed as she looked at Picasso.

No Mum, there are pressures being a dog, but not like the ones you are under. I wish things could always be the same, but I know things have to change. This is how we grow. I wish I could take the unhappiness away, Picasso said with concern.

Sara and Picasso tended to have a much longer walks in the evening.

C'mon, Mum, my feet are tired, time to go home. Picasso pulled on her lead.

'No, Picasso, just a little while longer. It's so peaceful and relaxing away from the house,' Sara stated.

I know, but you have to go back eventually. You have to face your problems. They just won't go away by themselves. You have to work through them, Picasso commented.

Sara and Picasso turned the last corner for home. After another few minutes, they were walking up the drive.

'Here comes more stress, Picasso,' Sara sighed as she entered the house.

Over the next few weeks, the tension in the house continued to rise, and some nasty words were said. Sara tried to spend as much time away from the house as possible. Tony grumbled all the time and retreated to the shed to tinker with things.

It feels like something is going to explode, Strife sensed.

It better not be the kitchen, Trouble added.

No, it's Mum and Dad. Something is not nice, and I feel bad things will happen. I can smell it all around, can you? Picasso looked towards the cats.

Yes, I feel the house will be changing soon. I feel this is the end. I wonder what they are going to do? Strife pondered.

They won't split us up, will they? Trouble asked.

What? Split us up? They wouldn't, would they? Picasso said.

It has been known to happen. They call it separation. It's when things are never the same again and we don't spend time as a family anymore. Strife crouched down.

Separate. So, it means living separate? We won't ever see each other again? That's sad. Trouble shook her head.

How do we stop it? Picasso asked in earnest.

I don't think it can be stopped. Sometimes, I think it might be better if they are away from each other. They might get along better. Sometimes, it's the best option. Strife was ready for a nap.

'I've had enough with you; I can't live like this anymore. We need to part. We're two different people now,' Sara said to Tony one night.

'It's all that study you are doing, putting ideas in your head. Everything was fine before. You changed because of going to university. I bet you can't even get a job out of it,' Tony snapped back.

'Nothing was fine before. I had a very poor paying job and we were just living paycheck to paycheck. I can't do this any longer. I need to do things with my life. We haven't been living – just going through the motions and existing,' Sara retorted.

'Nah, it's this learning stuff – putting weird things into your head. Everything was fine before you started this study stuff. Now, you have a large debt to pay off as well,' Tony arrogantly stated.

'What do you care about paying bills? I organise and plan all the bills and when they need to be paid. They keep coming in – there's no rest,' Sara raised her voice.

'Oh, don't start, I help with the bills too. What do you think I am?' Tony challenged, puffing out his chest.

'Yeah? Well it seems all my wages go to keeping the house going. I never have any spare money left over for a holiday, or to fix the car or to do anything else.' Sara stood with her hands on her hips, ready for confrontation.

'You're so annoying sometimes. You pick and pick and pick. It would send anyone to drink.' Tony knew Sara was ready to explode.

'Go ahead! At least I'd have some peace and quiet here, and not need to listen to you grumble all the time. It's depressing,' Sara answered back.

'I'm depressing? What about you? You don't do anything except do that study. The house is getting into a mess – all because of you,' Tony pointed with his arms to the state of the dining room table.

'I'm not the only one living here. There are two of us. Why don't you pull your weight? I can't live like this anymore. I'm done. I'm going to bed,' Sara retreated to the spare bedroom, where she had been sleeping for the past several months.

That was a nasty argument. Picasso hung her head.

There are several types of arguments: yelling, screaming, punching, kicking, biting, or even silence. Either way, it's not nice, Strife chattered.

Will they ever be nice to each other again? Trouble wondered.

I don't think so. I think there are too many long-term issues that can't be fixed. Some nasty words were thrown at each other that I think hit the truth mark. Strife started grooming her sister.

So, will this go on forever? Trouble returned the grooming, as she had found a hidden grass seed in her sister's coat.

I don't think it will, but life for us won't be the same ever again, Strife mumbled through the fur.

What about Mum and Dad? What's going to happen to all of us? Picasso shook.

We'll just have to wait and see. Strife continued to groom.

The next day, Sara came home from work and said to Tony in a deadpan voice, 'Get a lawyer. My lawyer is sending you paperwork. I've tried to do a fifty-fifty split. If you drag it out, the lawyers' fee will increase.'

Over the next few weeks, an unnatural silence descended on the house. Both Sara and Tony kept to themselves and no longer shared meals, or time. Sara started sprucing and cleaning the house, ready for the separation.

Is this how it's going to be? Nobody talking? The tension is still there, but this silence is deafening. If they were shouting, at least they would be talking, Picasso whimpered.

We still don't know what's going to happen. They're not talking at all. Silence is terrifying. It's like neglect, Trouble said.

They won't split us up, will they? Strife questioned.

What if they do? I'm scared. Trouble quivered.

Do we decide, or do we wait for them to decide? Picasso asked.

Well, I think we should stick together, no matter what. We've spent too much time together to be split up. What do you think? Strife questioned the others.

You're my sister. We were womb mates and I'm staying right by your side no matter what. Trouble cuddled next to Strife.

Both cats stared at Picasso, who had tears welling up in her eyes.

I think we all stick together, even you, Picasso. We belong together, Strife warmly said as Picasso crept closer to the cats.

Nightmares of being pulled apart from her surroundings, home, and sisters haunted Picasso.

'Where will you go? How will you manage?' Tony asked Sara one night.

'I got that job I applied for. They know I'm not finished my degree but they're willing to take me on. I'm starting at a more substantial amount than what I've been getting. I'll even be able to save some money for a holiday. I've found a unit to rent closer to the city and work. Things are finally going my way,' Sara commented.

'What's going to happen with the animals?' Tony questioned.

'What do you think? Who's been looking after them all this time? Who feeds them, who takes them for walks, who takes them to the vet, who cleans their bowls?' Sara stated with her hands on her hips.

'I do this stuff too, you know. What if they want to stay?' Tony challenged.

'Ask them. If they want to stay, let them. But I have a strange feeling they will want to come with me,' Sara offered.

Yeah, we get to choose, Trouble said with glee.

It's a tough decision, to stay or go, Strife added.

I'm torn, but I feel I need to be with Mum. She does everything with me, and for me. I think I need to be with Mum, Picasso admitted.

Okay, all in agreeance, stick with Mum? Strife nodded to her two sisters.

Just as long as all the food keeps coming like usual, Trouble added.

Trouble, who do you think gets your food most of the time? Strife was exasperated.

Oh, yeah, stick with Mum. Trouble beamed.

'Well then, we shall see tomorrow when the removalist comes for my stuff. If they want to come with me, they will. I've got to finish packing.' Sara moved to her empty boxes and started to fill them with her things.

The next morning, the removalists arrived, and Sara directed them to her items, which they packed on the truck in no time at all. Checking for the final time, Sara noticed all three animals waiting for her at her car.

'Well, I suppose you're coming with me. Just let me get your food and bowls. I'll leave a note for Tony.' Sara retreated to the house to grab the pet's food, bowls, blankets and other items. A quick note was left for Tony. Sara, Trouble, Strife and Picasso were loaded into the car for their next chapter in life.

Chapter 25: We Begin Again

Sara parked at her new rental town house moments before the removalists arrived. The smart brick and cream coloured aluminium trim would keep looking good for a long time. She quickly herded the animals into the downstairs toilet, placed a bowl of fresh water and a mat, and shut the door. They would be safe and secure in there until the removalists were finished. They took a remarkably short time bringing in furniture and boxes. After they left, Sara looked around at her new place. The floor tiles gleamed in the sunlight from the windows.

'Is this all I have to show from a lifetime? A few sticks of furniture and a couple dozen boxes? Well, I guess it's time to begin,' Sara said to herself.

Making sure the house was safe, she allowed the animals out of the bathroom. Sara started to unpack her meagre items and found a new home for them. Everything was so different here; the animals took their time sniffing and exploring every inch of their new surroundings.

There's been a dog here before. I can smell him. He was big, and hairy too, Picasso deduced.

Only the one, but I think there was also a cat here too. It's very faint, but definitely a cat, Strife added.

These floors are hard to grip. They're slippery and it will be hard to stop if you're running fast, Trouble reasoned.

Since when do you ever run fast? Maybe when it's dinner time? Strife smirked.

At least there are familiar smells from the lounge and dining table. It's nice to have something from the old place, Picasso piped up.

It's got this really big room at the back. Mum's furniture will look tiny in here, as Strife entered the back area.

Hey, the kitchen is tucked into the corner. Come on, Mum's put some food down, Trouble shouted out.

It took the rest of the day to explore the house and sniff the outside air. Sara kept the cats inside for several days to make sure they were safe and got used to their new home. Picasso could go out on regular walks and explore her new area. She brought back news as soon as Sara turned her back.

'Okay kitty cats, time to visit the back courtyard. I know it's a different one from the one you had before, but I'm sure there will be lots of smells and fun things to do here. It's not as big, in fact it's tiny compared to what you are used to, but it's safe and secure for you.' Sara slid the patio doors open.

Trouble and Strife took a few tentative steps outside. They had spent the last few days peering out the glass door at the yard, but now they had a chance to really see and smell it. Picasso barged through and showed the cats the most interesting things and her favourite spots. The cats followed Picasso and daily routines were settled quickly.

I'm glad our days are working out well. I hate too much change, Strife admitted as she breathed in the backyard air.

Food and sleep, what more do we need? Trouble added.

I think we made a good choice coming with Mum. Now I understand what you mean by being a companion dog. I help Mum negotiate all the broken pavement when we are walking, so she doesn't trip. It's a busy road, but a different busy from before, Picasso informed.

There are so many houses here – you can only see houses, no empty spaces,

Trouble offered.

I guess this is what they call a city, Strife thought.

They do have some grass areas, but they are only small, Picasso offered.

Still, I think we'll be okay here in the house and yard. We're getting older, so we don't need a lot of room to move, Strife said.

There seems to be so much movement at the front, all sorts of strange people coming and going, Trouble stated.

A train station is nearby. A train is a big bus-like thing that runs on a special road just for trains. People go on it and off it. It takes them places, Picasso explained.

So that's why it's so noisy. It feels like thunder shaking the whole house, and me. It feels like my insides are being shifted about, Strife said, her back legs wobbling slightly.

I think it's just the trains, Trouble comforted.

Strife looked at her two sisters, then headed off for a nap. She staggered and lost her balance a few times, but finally made it to a spot. She ended up dragging her back legs into a ball.

It's more than the trains, something is happening inside me. It feels really weird – like rushing and then sudden stopping. I don't think it's good, Strife mumbled to herself, her words not clear.

Well, despite the noisy trains, it's much quieter here. Less conversation out of Mum, Trouble said.

I guess there's no one else to talk to. She could always talk to us, Picasso said hopefully.

The animals had their naps and dreamt about trains taking people places. Trouble snuggled up near Strife, like she always did. Picasso was in her basket, keeping a watch over the kitchen and hallway area. Their inbuilt alarm clock roused the animals from their sleep, just about when Sara usually came home. Greeting her was Picasso and Trouble.

'Where's Strife? Is she still sleeping?' Sara asked.

Picasso and Trouble escorted Sara to where Strife was napping, only to find her shaking uncontrollably.

'Strife, what's happening?' Sara rushed to her side and crouched low to pat her.

Strife? What's going on? The trains are not going right now, stop shaking, Trouble called out.

Something is wrong with her, she's not teasing. She's ill. Smell her, Picasso warned.

'Strife, what's happening to you?' Sara caressed her body, and the shakes and tremors lessened.

Groggily, Strife opened her eyes and tried to focus on her surroundings. She tried to talk but could not make any sound. Her world was still spinning, and it took several more minutes for her to focus on Trouble, Picasso and Mum. Strife tried to get up but fell to the ground.

'Something's not right. I'm taking you to the vet,' Sara said.

Sara gently picked Strife up and wrapped her in a towel. Grabbing her keys, she left the house. Sara drove as fast as she dared to the vet's. Strife was placed comfortably on the passenger seat; Sara made several glances at Strife during the trip. Once at the vet's, Sara darted in, just as they were starting to shut for the night.

'Please, help me, my cat started shaking and trembling. Something is seriously wrong. Please see her,' Sara presented her bundle of towel and cat to the vet.

The vet led Sara to the examination room, pointing at the table. Taking out his stethoscope, he listened to Strife's body.

'How long has this been going on for?' the vet asked.

'I don't know. I've just come home from work and saw her like this,' Sara admitted.

'Hmm, how old is she? What has her health been like?' the vet continued to ask questions.

'She's sixteen, and she's never had any health issues before. She gets regular worm, flea and tick routines. What's happening?' Sara was worried.

Just then, Strife had another fit of shakes and trembles. Her eyes rolled back into her head, her tongue fell out of her mouth, and her whole body convulsed in spasms. The vet felt certain areas of her tummy area and checked her heart and face again. Strife started choking on her own dribble.

'I think she's having a stroke caused by a blood clot somewhere. She can't use her back legs; they have no more feeling, see? This clot is doing irreparable damage. At her age, most treatments won't work,' the vet confessed.

'Oh my, the poor cat. Is she in pain? Are you sure nothing else can help?' Sara pleaded.

'She's had good innings. She is struggling with this. See the tension in her face? It's controlling her now. The stroke will take her very soon,' The vet stroked Strife.

Sara pondered this news for a few seconds, and cupped Strife's head. Strife's whole face was skewed in a tight knot. This was unfair. She should not be going through this.

'Okay. Put her out of her misery. Let her be at peace,' Sara told the vet.

Tears were streaming from Sara's eyes. The vet took a vial out of the refrigerator, picked up a needle and filled it with the green-coloured liquid.

'It's for the best. It must be very uncomfortable for her having these seizures,' the vet comforted.

The vet inserted the needle; Strife's tension eased and her whole body relaxed. The vet listened to Strife's heart and checked her pulse. There was nothing.

'I want to take her home with me. The other two animals need to say goodbye. I'll bury her myself. Thank you.' Sara wrapped Strife in the towel, paid at the counter and left the vet's office.

Once home, Sara gently placed Strife in her towel on the back patio, allowing Trouble and Picasso to view her. Sara grabbed the garden spade and began to dig a hole in the garden.

What did she do to her? She's not moving, Trouble sniffed.

I think she's dead. Just like Big Bro. I think it was her time, Picasso said somberly.

I thought she was teasing us with the shaking. But it was real? She was really sick, wasn't she? Trouble asked Picasso.

Yes, I think she was. She didn't let on how sick she was. But I could smell something awful happening in her body. Poor Strife. Picasso looked towards Sara digging a hole, remembering how it was with her Big Bro.

I've lost my sister. I need some time to myself. Trouble retreated to the house.

Picasso stayed for a few minutes until she saw Sara coming towards Strife. Picasso knew what was going to happen next and made her quick exit into the farthest area of the house and hid under the bed. She could not bear another memorial. Maybe Sara would like some comfort tonight. She's lost many things: Big Bro, her home, her relationship, and now Strife.

Maybe this is what I'm supposed to do now, comfort and protect Sara, Picasso reflected.

That evening, Sara, Trouble and Picasso cuddled on the lounge. No words were spoken; group sadness was understood. Over the next few days, this heavy veil slowly lifted, and life continued. As Picasso was not close to Strife, her grief did not last as long, but she still vowed to be a companion dog to Sara.

In the middle of the night a month or two later, Picasso sensed something terrible and frightening. She jumped onto Sara's bed, waking her up. Picasso lay down at the foot of the bed and let out a low growl that shook the bed.

'What's up, Picasso? This isn't your usual behaviour. Go back to bed,'

Sara said sleepily.

The bedside clock said three forty-seven a.m. Just then, Sara and Picasso heard the distinctive sound of the front gate latch opening. Picasso stood up, all her hackles standing on end. Her body was tense, and her growling becoming more ferocious. She peeled back her gums to show her big canine teeth. She started snarling and snapping. Sara had never seen the little dog turn into such an angry, ready-to-fight animal. Sara would hate to be the person at the other end of Picasso's aggression. Fully alert now, both Sara and Picasso heard someone trying to open the screen door.

The sleepy night exploded into a torrent of abuse from Picasso. She launched herself off the bed and ran to the door, barking in a deep voice. Spittle was flying from her mouth – she intended to fight to the very end. Sara crept to the front door and noticed a dark blur running away from the house. Picasso still trying to get through the door to attack, Sara marvelled that her little dog could turn so savage and violent to an intruder.

Shining red and blue lights came to a halt at the neighbour's house: the police had arrived. They searched around the town house's side passage and caught one culprit and threw him into the back of the van.

Sara slowly ventured out onto the porch; Picasso was sniffing where the intruder had been. Picasso got a good indication of who the person was but was quickly whisked into Sara's arms to watch the action unfolding. Picasso sniffed the air towards the police van.

They have the wrong person, Mum. The one in the van is not the same one on the porch. Be careful, he's still out there, Picasso warned.

Picasso's senses were on full alert, she continued to sniff the air and look around. Her warning growl could be clearly heard. He was still out there.

Mum, he's not far. I think he's across the road in the bushes. See over there? They are moving and there is little breeze. He's over there. That's him. Picasso tried to point with her nose, her growls becoming more audible.

The police continued to look around the houses, and in front gardens, anywhere someone could hide. Picasso let out a deeper, louder growl and started to bare her teeth as she snapped and snarled. The noise echoed in the night air towards the bushes across the road. Picasso's hackles rose again. Hearing the growl, the police swung their powerful torches towards the noise and blinded Sara and Picasso standing on their porch. The police saw the dog in Sara's arms and looked to where the dog was staring and growling. They swung the beam of the torch to the bushes across the street and picked up on the slight movement. The second policeman started towards the bushes as the first showered the bush in the torch's beam. Running towards the bush, there was a short tussle before the police caught and restrained the unsavoury thief and escorted him to the back of the wagon.

Picasso sniffed the night air again. All okay, they have them all. No other issues, her job was done and she relaxed in Sara's arms.

Don't mess with me, punk. I will keep my family, and especially Mum, safe. I am Chihuahua. You have been warned. Punk. Hail Chihuahua, Picasso puffed out.

The police left and Sara and Picasso returned to the house, ensuring all the doors and windows were fully locked and secure. The next day, Sara presented Picasso with a lamb shank.

'Thank you for protecting me last night, Picasso. Enjoy. I'll have to see if I can put you on my insurance as a guard dog,' Sara said fondly.

Chapter 26: Things That Creep Up on You

The pattern of city life was very similar to country life: the birds waking up and chirping; the heavy trucks doing their deliveries, picking up rubbish or getting ready for the day. Public buses and trains would become more frequent, ready for the morning rush, and people would begin milling about on their way to their daily routines. Sara, Picasso and Trouble soon settled into their own routines: getting up, going outside, eating, saying goodbye to Sara, napping until Sara returned home at the end of the day. The morning routine was then repeated almost exactly at night: getting up, going outside, eating, cuddling with Sara, napping.

Both Picasso and Trouble hibernated during the day, with no other stimulation happening.

I'm so exhausted doing nothing. All my energy is used to eat and sleep, Trouble chatted to Picasso.

I know what you mean. I've been to Sara's work once; all she does is sit at a desk or talk to people. How boring is that? She must miss us. As soon as she gets home, she plays with us and does things with us. I think Sara has to have more play in her life, Picasso reasoned.

Too energetic for me – play. I'm too old to play anymore, Trouble confessed.

Yeah, but you get pats and cuddles, don't you? Picasso offered.

And I love every minute of it. My old body is very tired and sore, so that eases the aches and pains. Trouble started to purr.

We're all getting older – it's part of life, Picasso commented and looked at her many grey hairs.

Some of us are older faster. Don't forget I have a lot of years on you to start with. I think I was six or seven when you came along, Trouble thought.

Don't remind me. You and your sister were horrible to me. Picasso did not dare speak Strife's name in case it upset Trouble.

You were an annoying young pup who did not understand the rules of the household or the pecking order. It took you a long time to understand things, Trouble stated.

If you were nicer to me, I might have learned quicker, Picasso retaliated.

I'm too tired to argue or talk. I'm off to sleep, Trouble sighed as she curled up into a ball. She shut her eyes and was fast asleep in no time.

Picasso retreated to her bed and curled up by herself and had her nap too. She tried not to remember her early life with the cats and concentrated on other happy things.

Our bodies are made up of senses: sight, hearing, touch, taste, smell. When one sense goes, usually the other ones pick up the slack. This started happening more and more for Trouble. Her hearing started to go, and she often had difficulty hearing Sara's car coming home and Sara calling out to her. Trouble would often wake up from her nap as a beautiful sensation of relaxing strokes on her body permeated her dreams. It took Trouble several minutes for her dream to fade, but the sensations were still there. Slowly coming out of her slumber, reality started to kick in.

Trouble, wake up, Mum's home. Picasso was excited to see Sara and was looking forward to going outside for a walk.

Trouble woke with a start and opened her eyes to see Picasso standing near her, and Sara's hand stroking her body.

'Wakey wakey, sleepyhead. I hope you had a good dream,' Sara said.

What? Are you home? Is it time to get up? I didn't hear you! Trouble blurted as she got to her feet, stretched, yawned and wandered to the back door and the yard outside.

Trouble spent the next hour or so sniffing the air, inspecting the garden and having a nap in her favourite spot in the warm afternoon sun.

During this time, Sara and Picasso had their afternoon walk. Picasso often argued and discussed at length which way to go with Sara. Picasso would win most of the time. Picasso regularly marvelled at the new smells and the familiar old smells on her specific routes, as if committing them to memory. She often became intolerant of meeting neighbourhood dogs and their human companions.

C'mon, Mum. I don't want to talk today; I just want to walk. I need to keep going or my legs will cease up, Picasso begged Sara as she continued to talk to Jill and her dog, Freddy.

'I think I'm being told off. She often tells me off when I stop and talk to other people. Gotta go.' Sara farewelled Jill and Freddy.

'That was a bit rude. I was talking, and you pulled me away,' Sara scolded Picasso.

I'm done talking. I want to walk. We've talked enough to them, Picasso retorted, and they continued their walk.

At home, the daily routine of feeding Trouble and Picasso began. Sara started preparing green vegetables for her evening meal.

Glad we have the good stuff, imagine wanting to eat green vegetables all the time? Trouble mumbled through a mouthful of food.

It's good for her; her coat, skin and hair glow much better. But she always puts some meat with it too. I wonder what it will be tonight? Picasso powered through her food bowl.

I'm just concentrating on my dinner. I can always look at Mum's coat and hair and skin later. I'm busy. Trouble continued to eat.

That evening, Sara, Trouble and Picasso snuggled on the lounge, watching a program on Indigenous peoples of the world and social injustices. Sara stroked Trouble with her left hand, and stroked Picasso with her right hand for a few minutes, until both nodded off to sleep.

I'm too tired to watch the television today, Trouble murmured.

The screen is getting blurry too. I'd like to listen, but Mum has the volume down real low. Picasso yawned.

I can't hear anything at all anymore. Night night. Trouble started to snooze and snore.

Picasso moved to the arm rest and spread out so that she was not touching Sara. Sara moved too much. Maybe she needed to do more walking and less talking. Picasso's dreams were filled with visions of trying to get Sara to walk more and talk less.

One day, Trouble did not wake from her afternoon nap. Picasso was both saddened and happy. Now, she had the whole house to herself and did not have to share anything with anybody, not even Sara. But she did miss the company. Picasso tried to comfort Sara as best as possible.

Picasso had seen so much grief, loss and death in her life: moving away from her birth family; finding new places to live and new faces to greet; losing her Big Bro; leaving Tony behind; losing Strife, and now, her sister Trouble. She felt her bones aching along with her heart. Sometimes, she could not hear things, and other times she could. A cloudy orb was hovering in front of her eyes, and she had trouble looking at things. At first, this scared her: was she really seeing what she thought she was seeing? She tried to move her head up and down and all around to see beyond this haze. What was worse, Sara continued to talk to people and other dogs on their afternoon walks.

This time is my time, Mum, Picasso would huff. She vowed to keep the walks moving in hopes of not meeting as many people.

'Oooh. What a lovely dog. He looks very old. How old is he?' a passer-by would ask.

'She's sixteen,' Sara would comment.

'He looks very good for an old dog,' the passer-by would comment.

'She is doing very well for an old dog, despite the cataracts and hearing loss. She, we, take every day as it comes,' Sara corrected.

I'm a girl dog. Why does everyone think I'm a boy? Let's keep going. Do you have to tell everyone how old I am? It makes me feel older, Picasso argued with Sara and pulled her away.

'You're getting very cranky in your old age, aren't you, Picasso? Why do you continue to argue with me?' Sara questioned as they continued walking.

Hmmph, was all Picasso could say as the walk went on.

Chapter 27: Soapbox

I'm tired of this sitting here doing nothing, let's go out, Picasso told Sara off.

'I'm busy typing here, we'll go in a few minutes,' Sara promised.

Don't take too long. Picasso settled down on her cushion by the desk.

Sara continued to type on her computer. After checking some details, and organisiong her desk, Sara shut down the computer.

'Okay, let's go.' Sara grabbed the lead.

Both Sara and Picasso took long walks through streets, through a park, and up and over a foot bridge, spending time chatting to people and sniffing new smells. It was just what Sara needed to clear her head.

'We must be careful with this dog, Picasso. She's been cruelly treated with a previous family and now lives with her foster mum. Bev is trying to work with the dog to regain trust in humans and other dogs to feel safe again. She's a rescue animal,' Sara warned.

Why do people treat their pets so horribly? I can't even imagine what terrible things they went through. Picasso shook her head.

'These animals need a lot of time, care, support and patience with their special human to get them from near-death and on the edge to a basic stage. I don't understand why people treat their pets so bad. I'm so lucky you came to our family. I've seen so many cases of neglect, it's heart breaking,' Sara continued.

If people don't like animals, why do they get them in the first place? They wouldn't like it if we did horrible things to them, would they? I still remember Betty who was chained to a tree. She didn't have a good life. Picasso stated.

'There are laws that protect companion animals, but there are so many cases that go unnoticed, and it costs a lot of money to prosecute. These animals do not deserve to be abused and neglected at all. That is no life for them. Luckily, there are special people like Bev who take the time to unravel their traumas and help them on the road to recovery,' Sara beamed.

There are so many selfless people who help and protect animals in all shapes and sizes. Sara reflected that this mirrored her new career as a HR representative after studying at university. Concepts of tolerance, acceptance, respect, inclusion, and a fight for those marginalised in the community was the way to live life.

How do we help to stop this treatment? Picasso asked.

'If people would only do the right thing: purchase from a registered breeder, not backyard farms; look after their pets; have them desexed; attend regular vet checks, immunisation and care; have them microchipped and socialised in the community. If you don't like animals or don't want to care for them properly, don't get them. C'mon, let's go home,' Sara stated.

Sara was lost in her own thoughts of all the ways to safeguard pets and how easy it was to care for them. She would never understand why some people mistreated animals. Perhaps they had no respect for themselves?

Later that night, Sara scrolled the internet and investigated animal rights and welfare.

'Hey, Picasso, it says here that we should treat animals with compassion, empathy and respect. This follows a golden rule of cultural ethics, and that we think they are like us. I mean, it makes sense as we include them in our everyday life. Some even take out pet insurance and we often call you 'our fur baby.' Many people treat animals as part of their family, and rightly so. It goes on to say what animal cruelty is: ignorance, neglect, intent, and endorsed cruelty.' Sara continued to read the screen.

I'm so glad I came to you, and the rest of the family. I am one lucky dog, Picasso sighed. Picasso put her head down and thought about all that she'd received: the good food, fresh water, shelter, comfort, safety and respect, no pain nor punishment, care, and the freedom to be herself. She shuddered to think others had never experienced this treatment.

Sara marvelled at Picasso, as every day was a bonus. At over sixteen years, she had outlived her expected life span.

Everyone can live a long life if you look after yourself, get regular exercise, eat healthy, live a stress-free life, be kind and reflective, share your life with others, and have no major physical ailments. Having a pet enriches our lives, teaches us to be tolerant and accepting, and caring and loving to others; but most importantly, provides us with entertainment and companionship.

Sara appreciated the time her pets had spent with her, and the many lessons they had taught her. Picasso's white face was merging with the rest of her body and legs. Her walks were becoming shorter as her arthritis ached.

Sara continued to reflect that companion animals gave so much: cuddles, kisses, time. They almost never talked back and always took the time to listen unconditionally. They appreciated the little things in life and didn't ask for much. They bring down stress levels as they seemed to understand how we're feeling. Some dogs even feel the changes in their owners, like when they're feeling blue. They just sit by our side, and comfort us in their own special way. Just having someone there for us means so much. Picasso was no different. She seemed to sense what Sara needed and how to sort things out.

Sara thought back to the many dogs and cats she has had throughout her life, and the joys they have brought her. Something must be done to capture this bond. Animals teach us to enjoy life, and all other living things. Big Bro hoped to leave us in a better place, and Sara thought he did. He passed on his wisdom, kindness and perspective to others to share. Even though they are no longer with us, they will always be in our memories. Nobody can take this away from us.

Perhaps there is a way to capture these lives and to help others to remember unconditional love and acceptance? Perhaps the lessons animals teach us can be followed to make our lives better. Perhaps we can make a difference and leave a positive mark in society for future generations. Perhaps the world can be a better place.

Sara pondered all this and glanced down at Picasso resting on her cushion. Perhaps these stories could help others.

Sara started a new word document and began typing Big Bro's memories and antics. Sara also understood she needed to include the other animals and people who had enriched her life. Picasso woke, shuffled and fluffed the cushion before she settled down again. She gave Sara a dirty look. How much did Picasso understand? Sara sighed and continued to type. The working title of her story emerged on the screen: 'The Art of Picasso.'

The End

Acknowledgements

The animals in this book were humanely treated and cared for. They all lived to at least sixteen years. All avenues of care were offered.

This story was supposed to be about my Kelpie, Big Bro. He was an exceptional dog, and I wanted to write about him, but a little black dog kept interrupting and bossing me about.

I'd like to thank all the people (and cats and dogs too) who have assisted in some way to make this dream come true; but especially to the young people who told me, 'I just want someone to listen to me without making judgements or giving me adult advice. I don't trust them, but I trust my dog.'

I would like to thank the people who supported me through this journey – I would be lost without you. Jasmine for editing, Chrissy for art, Graham for mentoring and publishing, Deb for listening and encouraging and Vic who read this first.

This is a work of fiction, all characters are made up.

About the Author

Sue lives in the Hunter Valley of New South Wales and enjoys the open spaces and diversity of landscape. Sue combines her degrees in Social Science, Creative Writing and work within the community to explore human conditions and experiences. She brings a variety of lived experiences and other elements to each piece of writing, and is passionate about community, surrounding environments, addressing mental health issues and all the souls she meets (both two- and four-footed).

www.ingramcontent.com/pod-product-compliance
Lightning Source LLC
Chambersburg PA
CBHW020325010526
44107CB00054B/1977